PRAISE FOR

Byline

Cristi Hegranes's *Byline* upends the idea of foreign reporting as historically practiced and thoughtfully offers better, accurate ways forward. Her oft-amusing examples of "parachute journalism" are eye-opening, expose the dangers and limitations of mainstream media, and inspire all of us to do better. Where this book most shines is in proffering solutions, such as how communities can tell their own stories or how audience feedback can be revolutionary. There's nothing parochial about Hegranes's vision for local news; indeed, it's an essential guide to committing and consuming journalism in the new world order.

S. MITRA KALITA
CEO, URL Media

Byline is an essential book for anyone who cares about international journalism. Drawing on seventeen years of experience building and running one of the most transformative models for journalism to be found anywhere in the world, Hegranes is uniquely positioned to explain what's wrong with the current system and, most importantly, how it can genuinely be improved.

DAVID BORNSTEIN
Cofounder, Solutions Journalism Network

Byline is many things—prescient, erudite, and timely—but it is especially an affirmation of the value of journalism when it is done well.

KHADIJA PATEL
Journalist in residence, International Fund for Public Interest Media

Byline

CRISTI HEGRANES

WITH SETH LIBBY

Byline

How Local Journalists Can Improve the
Global News Industry and Change the World

Advantage | Books

Published by Advantage, Charleston, South Carolina.
Member of Advantage Media.

ADVANTAGE is a registered trademark, and the Advantage colophon is a trademark of Advantage Media Group, Inc.

Printed in the United States of America.

10 9 8 7 6 5 4 3 2 1

ISBN: 978-1-64225-687-1 (Hardcover)
ISBN: 978-1-64225-686-4 (eBook)

Library of Congress Control Number: 2023903142

Cover design by David Taylor.
Layout design by Matthew Morse.

This publication is designed to provide accurate and authoritative information in regard to the subject matter covered. It is sold with the understanding that the publisher is not engaged in rendering legal, accounting, or other professional services. If legal advice or other expert assistance is required, the services of a competent professional person should be sought.

To my son, Henry, whose magic lights the world

and

to the reporters of Global Press, past, present, and future,
with gratitude for your stories that help us see the world as it truly is.
—C. H.

To Liza and Lucas.
—S. L.

Contents

PART I
Systemic Failure

Acknowledgments

A single bracelet does not jingle.
—CONGOLESE PROVERB

Through their love, support, wisdom, and generosity, these people have given breath to the dream that is Global Press. Without them, Global Press, and this book, would not have been possible.

Laxmi Parthasarathy, who is a powerhouse COO and a kind friend who always pushes me to be better.

Amy Low and Brooke Runnette, who made this book possible with their coaching and by including me in the transformational Emerson Collective Dial Fellowship.

Kudzai Mazvarirwofa, for fact checking this book and sharing your powerful story.

Bennett Hanson, for your commitment to research, precision, and holding power to account. Your research, as always, was invaluable here.

The brilliant Global Press reporters who lent their voices and their stories to this book: Apophia Agiresaasi, Mar Garcia, Khorloo Khukhnokhoi, Merveille Kavira Lungehe, Shilu Manandhar, Gamu Masiyiwa, Linda Mujuru, Edna Namara, Noella Nyirabihogo, Avigaí Silva, and Aline Suárez del Real. I am endlessly grateful for each of you.

The incredible Global Press staffers who lent their perspectives and their keen eyes to this book: Terry Aguayo, Allison Braden, Shanté Cosme, Katie Myrick, Shazdeh Omari, Manori Wijesekera, and Celia Wu.

Marissa Revilla, *la gran dama de Global Press*, who has been with me every step of this journey since 2006. Your voice and your courage are unmatched.

My industry colleagues and other experts who offered their wisdom and their words to these pages: Carroll Bogert of *The Marshall Project*, David Folkenflik of NPR, Bobby Ghosh of Bloomberg, Steve Hanke of Johns Hopkins University, Sara Just of *PBS NewsHour*, Krista Karch, Nicholas Kristof of the *New York Times*, Moky Makura of Africa No Filter, Lauren Williams of Capital B, and Lesley Wroughton.

Kate Gardiner and the Grey Horse team, who helped me prepare for this moment.

Lane Bove, John Mecklin, and Carol Sternhell, who are incredible educators who helped me understand the responsibility and the social justice potential of journalism.

Kelly McBride and Keith Woods, who have served as mentors and supporters since my first days in the profession.

Deborah Stone, whose humble generosity knows no equal.

Emily Kaiser, whose friendship and support constantly propel Global Press to new heights. I am in awe of the casual way in which you inflict positive change on the world.

Kathy Im, who was the first to take a big bet on Global Press. I am forever grateful for your belief in what was, and continues to be, possible.

Michelle Swenson, who has been a fabulous board chair, and to every member of the Global Press board, past and present, for your leadership and support.

Elaine Nonneman, Katrin Wilde, Bill and Sue Gee, Annie Mize, Benno Friedman, Dan Austin, Sybil Masquelier, Susie Tompkins Buell, and Belinda Muñoz, for more than a decade of support.

Wynnette LaBrosse, who is an unmatched cheerleader, risk taker, thinker, and friend.

Mary Galeti, who helped give shape to Duty of Care and who has given support, friendship, and breakfast burritos for years.

My dad, who was Global Press's first supporter and someone who constantly helps me understand the world better.

My whole family, Jon, Pei, Mom, Jeff, Carol, Parker, and of course, my Harper Xu, whom I love so much.

Meagan Demitz, who both lent her expertise to this book and has given me twenty-two years of transformational friendship.

Seth Libby, who was a powerful listener and an eloquent partner in this project.

And of course to my son, Henry, who makes me smarter, kinder, and better. And who is my forever reason to keep pushing for a more informed and inclusive world.

Preface

Local journalists can save the world.

That's not hyperbole. I know this because giving bylines to local journalists is my life's work. In 2006, I founded an international nonprofit news organization, Global Press, to train and employ local women journalists to cover the places mainstream news ignores—communities across Africa, Asia, Latin America, and the Caribbean. Over the last seventeen years, Global Press has worked with more than 250 local journalists. Together, they have produced thousands of profound stories that have quite literally changed the world. They have prompted law changes and spurred local movements. They have given local people access to lifesaving information, and they have helped millions to see the world differently. Their stories are dignified and precise. And they offer comprehensive coverage of complex and historically misunderstood places.

Our mission at Global Press is to change the static global narratives that mainstream media perpetuates and to increase access to accurate information in the communities where our reporters work. And that's my mission in this book as well. In the chapters ahead, you'll meet Global Press reporters from Sri Lanka to Zimbabwe. You'll see how their local access yields exceptional stories that help people everywhere to better understand the world and their places in it.

But this book isn't about Global Press. It's about how local journalists can provide a way forward for the entire journalism industry. And it's about why this moment is the right time for change.

The failure of journalistic institutions to provide the whole story, the stories that people most need, is a part of the reason news consumers have turned against news providers. The loss of trust in journalism is complex, but at heart, many consumers simply do not believe they're getting the whole story. And that is certainly true in international news.

This book tackles how we tell international stories and how we decide who gets to tell them. It advocates for taking small steps to change everything about how we cover the world, including the words we use in our stories. You may notice that certain common terms—America, Global South, third world, ethnic, the West, and so on—are either absent in these pages or used only to be made examples of. And above all, it insists that we take greater care to protect our most valuable assets: our reporters.

Many of the long-held ideas and assumptions about audience appetites for international news are challenged too. There is new and compelling data that suggests that people are overwhelmed by disaster narratives, and they want to better understand communities outside of their own. It's not that they don't care about the world; it's that they don't care for the way the world's stories are being told.

While I'm aware some of the ideas ahead may seem at first improbable and others unworkable, I ask only for the opportunity to prove what I have known now for seventeen years: local journalists can save the world—if we just give them the chance to.

Introduction

War. Poverty. Disaster. Disease.

It's how we've all been conditioned to see most of the world. International news readers are often introduced to people in global communities on their worst days. Why? Because journalists are only sent to report on African villages in moments of famine or into Middle Eastern homes in the midst of war.

Audiences are made to think that's the whole story. But it's not. It never is.

The consequences of these singular and reductionist stories are many—reinforcing global stereotypes, overemphasizing poverty, and perpetuating inequitable and inaccurate global narratives top the list.

The systems of international news gathering and reporting are broken. They are rooted in a colonial legacy that hasn't evolved— systems built upon sending elite outsiders into global communities to "get" their stories and the companion assumption that "those people" in "those places" cannot report the news themselves.

I know this system well. Being a traveling correspondent, or a parachute journalist, was my dream job. When I was a little girl, I used to imagine traveling the world, telling its stories. I committed myself from an early age to that aim—and I never wavered.

In 2004 I got what I thought was my big break. I was finishing my master's degree in journalism at New York University. In my final semester, with the help of my professor Carol Sternhell, I managed to turn a classroom assignment into the opportunity to go to Nepal to report on women's rights during the civil war. My first parachute.

It was the summer of 2004, and the civil war that began in 1996 still had a few years left in it. Arriving in Kathmandu, I bolted off the plane with a clear set of stories I wanted to tell and a list of editors to whom I planned to send my story pitches. I wasn't working for any one place, nor was I being paid for my time. Still, I was undaunted, convinced that these were my stories to tell. I had plans to visit women who had been imprisoned for having abortions and to meet the founder of Nepal's first and then-only LGBTQ+ center. I had plans to travel the countryside and tell stories of the health and human consequences of this war.

After being in country for only a few days, I found reality began to interfere with those plans—and the fantasy job I had spent decades building in my mind. For all my drive and good intentions, I'd never really thought through the logistics or the ethics of the work.

I didn't speak Nepali, except for a few phrases I'd learned from a tutor back in Queens before my trip. Parachute journalists work with translators and fixers, local reporters who assist the outsiders in securing sources and navigating logistics, all the time, and I intended to do the same. But because of the war and the sensitive nature of the stories, I had to use government-employed translators on some occasions. That meant that the government controlled everything I learned from the people I interviewed. In other cases my local translators were not allowed to accompany me, leaving me mostly unable to communicate with my sources. When I'd get back to the guest lodge at night, I would look at my notes, feeling certain of just one thing: I couldn't ethically put quotes around anything.

Not only was I unable to speak to sources directly, but many potential sources also were unwilling to share their experiences with an outsider. I quickly began to realize the true depth of my lack of access. Beyond my sources, I also lacked access in more fundamental ways: to social, historical, and political context. The conflict happening around me was complicated and unfamiliar to anyone outside Nepal. Everyone had a different version of what had happened before and what would happen next. I felt I was in no position to determine where reality lay.

There were a few other parachute journalists around from India and Europe who told me that this was just how the game was played. "You do your best, and that's better than nothing," I remember one Danish journalist telling me. Night after night, I found myself wondering if that was true.

It seemed my options were to tell the story poorly or leave it entirely untold. Both felt wrong.

Feeling on ever less certain ground, I left Kathmandu and decided to refocus my efforts in other, more rural, parts of the country. And that's where I really did hit upon a great story—I just couldn't tell it.

I traveled around, visiting numerous small villages. In one I lucked into meeting a woman named Pratima. She spoke a little English, which she said she picked up from her nieces who attended school in India. I had many questions for her. Atop my list was why the village was filled with only women, children, and a few elderly people. She told me this wasn't unusual. The men were all either fighting the war or working abroad in India or the Middle East.

A few days after I arrived, we were discussing the long distance between the village and the nearest health post. I had noticed the many women walking there each day. That's when Pratima told me about "love's disease," the name given to the illness some of the local women had developed in recent years. It seemed it was worse among women whose husbands worked abroad and only visited once a year or so. I asked Pratima if HIV testing was locally available. She'd never heard of the disease.

In 2004, UNAIDS reported just 715 cases of HIV in all of Nepal.[1] Testing and awareness remained extremely low. Talking to Pratima, I had a hunch HIV was the culprit here.

There it was: the story I felt sure I was meant to tell.

But the local women in the village felt otherwise. Even in the absence of data, I might have been able to build the story exclusively around the experiences of women with "love's disease," but just like in Kathmandu, I found that many of them were uncomfortable talking to me about their circumstances. Despite Pratima's best efforts, many would simply stare at me. Our communication lacked clarity and trust.

One afternoon, in a moment of utter frustration, I handed Pratima my notebook, and I asked her to take over. I asked her to write down the details and the context I couldn't get and to speak to the women who wouldn't speak to me.

Later, when I returned to Kathmandu on my way to India, I had her notes translated. As I read them over and over again, a realization swept over me—Pratima was a natural reporter. She asked brilliant questions and took amazing notes with key details about how long it took to reach the health post and the gossip discussed along the way.

---

1   UNAIDS, "Epidemiological Fact Sheets on HIV/AIDS and Sexually Transmitted Infections: Nepal," unaids.org, accessed February 2, 2023. https://data.unaids.org/publications/fact-sheets01/nepal_en.pdf.

Her words gave context and nuance where I had only scratched the surface.

I often tell this story at speaking events, and it's at this point that I usually jump to the big moment of enlightenment and the founding of my news organization. However, there's a short but important interlude that deserves mention here.

In an email I sent to my mom in August of 2004, I wrote, "This whole process doesn't make any sense. I'm the wrong person to be telling these stories."

I was heartbroken and deflated. And I was confused. I had conflicting feelings about what to do with Pratima's notes. I hadn't paid her to be my fixer, and I hadn't ensured that the women she quoted understood what I was planning to do with their words—publish them.

Ultimately, I never wrote the story. I packed up the notebook in my backpack, and I went home feeling certain that none of these stories were mine to tell.

After Nepal, I graduated from NYU with my masters, and I moved to San Francisco, where I took a job as a feature writer at *SF Weekly*. I was one of five feature reporters.

It was a cool job. *SF Weekly* had a nonassignment policy that allowed me to report on what I cared about most. I wrote about AIDS, terrorism, and migrant issues. I had the print cover once every five weeks.

I won a few awards and had just begun to settle in when I realized I had to go. This realization was partly the fault of my editor, John Mecklin. He was too good at his job. He was a teacher and coach, and he made me better with each story. But every time I got his notes, the seeds of my idea grew.

The truth was, I couldn't get Pratima and my Nepal experience out of my head. I was fixated on the equity issues baked into parachute journalism. I was troubled by the notion that people like me, with no context or authentic access, could just drop into a country and tell stories just because we presumed we had the power and the authority to do so.

So I quit. I immediately walked across the street to a bookstore, and I bought a NOLO guide on how to start a nonprofit organization. I was twenty-five, and I had decided to pursue an idea I'd developed for how to change international news. That idea became Global Press, a nonprofit news organization that builds independent news bureaus, staffed by local women reporters, in some of the world's least-covered places.

How Something Becomes the News

I have ambivalent feelings about that story, chiefly because it centers my experience. No matter how many times I tell it, Pratima is always a side character, whereas to me, she's the hero. She was an inspiration for what I believe is the way forward for all journalism: those with the most proximate access must become the storytellers of record. In other words, we must elevate local journalists to tell the stories of their communities to the world. Pratima had no training as a journalist, but the world is full of talented, trained local journalists who have the context and the access to transform our worldview. We just need to find new ways to give them larger platforms.

Still, I think there's value in telling my story because it highlights the mindset at the heart of international news—a mindset we need to change. Looking back, I am amazed how entitled I felt to the stories of people whose language I didn't speak, whose culture I barely understood, and whose social context often passed me by. This was the early

2000s, and we didn't use phrases like "recognizing privilege" back then, but in retrospect, that's precisely the tension I felt in my reporting.

International journalism is rooted in historically inequitable systems that prioritize the stories told by elite outsiders, whose reports are about people that they are never for. Nothing sums this up quite like a study done by a pair of Norwegian researchers, Johan Galtung and Mari Holmboe Ruge, in 1965. The report, The Structure of Foreign News, describes the criteria most often used in the development of international news stories:

- The more distant the nation, the more negative the event must be.
- The more culturally distant the theater, the more relevant must the event appear to be.
- The lower the rank of the person, the more unexpected the news has to be.
- The lower the rank of the nation, the higher the rank of the person must be.
- The lower the rank of the person, the more negative the actions of the person will have to be.[2]

That study is more than fifty years old. In the years since that study, just about everything in journalism has changed. We've changed the way we report news, the way we consume news, the way we publish news, and the way we pay for news. Everything is different—except this. The mindset of how international stories come to be is unchanged. And the outcomes—simplistic, unedifying, disaster-driven, victim-centered stories—are still the result.

---

2   Johan Galtung and Marl Holmboe Ruge, "The Structure of Foreign News,"
     Journal of Peace Research 2, no. 1, (October 2009), DOI: http://dx.doi.
     org/10.1177/002234336500200104.

The news industry still assumes that audiences only want to hear about another part of the world if something terrible is happening. It also assumes that if people want to hear those stories at all, they'll want to hear them from a name or face that looks like their own: someone who is able to frame the story in a way that suits the dominant worldview in a manner dramatic enough to hold our attention.

But this moment in human history calls for a different way. It calls for context, precision, and comprehensive coverage that allows us to better understand the world and our place in it.

Our world is more interconnected than ever before. Young people play video games with friends in Nigeria and Bolivia. They follow influencers from Cambodia and Nicaragua. They watch shows about South Korea and Egypt. Professionals work with businesses on every continent. Their products can't be sold if the parts aren't manufactured in Vietnam and assembled in Mexico.

Our world is much smaller than the world of 1965 when Galtung and Ruge studied how distant places only received coverage on their worst days. Today, readers deserve the whole story. And to deliver it, journalism needs a new system—one that prioritizes a different storyteller.

Change the Storyteller

It's no secret that the journalism industry has been slow to adapt to a changing landscape. Legacy institutions are still resistant to some of the most obvious solutions to rebuilding trust and engaging audiences. Root causes are still not being addressed.

So let's start by overhauling how we cover international news. We can use international news as a test case to prove that many of the solutions are easier than you think. These same solutions can then be grafted onto every other kind of coverage.

The steps required to produce dignified and precise international journalism that will better serve audiences aren't innovative; they are basic and can be summed up in a single word: proximity.

We can rebuild trust and increase access to accurate information by simply employing journalists with the greatest proximity to the story at hand. And from this simple notion, everything changes.

I'm well aware of the old logic that suggests we need objective outsiders to tell us stories from the rest of the world. But that argument, as you will see in the pages that follow, doesn't hold up today. The plain fact is that local journalists have access to the stories the world needs. This premise is at the core of the Global Press model.

I built Global Press to pioneer a different kind of journalism. We train and employ local women journalists in some of the world's least-covered places to provide comprehensive coverage of their communities for both local and global audiences. We publish news in seven languages and have local reporters stationed in more than three dozen global bureaus.

That was the big idea I couldn't shake back in 2004. No matter how I looked at it, international reporting clearly needed a new model. To tell stories that news consumers want and need, we need people who actually speak the local language. To help us understand what is happening on a deeper level, we need people who live in those communities and are representative of the local people. To change the story, we need to change the storyteller.

We can offer readers an insider's guide to the world. But to do that, we have to get beyond general assumptions of truth and get to locally verified accuracy.

Let me explain. Look up any legacy media story about sub-Saharan Africa, and nine times out of ten you'll find superficial descriptions of poverty. Parachute journalists use terms like "developing world" to imply poverty. They describe local women by the number of children they have and local men by the condition of their clothes. These details might be true, but they don't often represent a person, place, or event accurately.

Take, for instance, the story that launched the Global Press Style Guide, a free online resource that offers rules for language choices that ensure dignity and precision in international journalism. A few years after Global Press launched, a copy editor inserted what seemed like an innocent dependent clause into an article about a farmer in rural Kenya. The added words labeled the farmer as being "among the poorest of the poor, because he lived on less than a few dollars a day."

The copy editor relied on World Bank data to draw this conclusion, not realizing that this farmer lived in a largely cashless society. So global standards of poverty based on access to cash didn't apply. In fact, to a farmer who was rich in noncash assets, this framing was nonsensical.

The copy editor's well-intentioned addition was true—in a way. By the World Bank's definition, the man was among the world's poorest because he didn't have access to even a small amount of cash on a daily basis. But it wasn't accurate.

The farmer in the story had land, livestock, and crops. In his community he was wealthy. He had a nice home, and his kids were all enrolled in private school. It was the Kenyan reporter of the piece who caught the change and corrected it. She knew the difference, and it was an important one.

Each region, country, and town is replete with dynamics as unique and complex as in that village. Understanding those dynamics requires something the parachute journalist can't often attain—access.

They lack access to sources across the entire community and context that explains the nuances of that community.

So the theory of change here is both simple and obvious—if we rely on the people who understand those dynamics best to tell the story, we not only provide the international news consumer with a more accurate worldview, but we also offer the local sources the dignity of being able to recognize themselves in stories. And those two things form the beginnings of rebuilding trust in journalism.

Readers want news they trust so they can understand the world. To understand the world, they need more than the standard, superficial stories of tragedy that international journalism usually provides. We have a lot to learn from the rest of the world, and readers know that.

The value of changing our news paradigm can't be overstated. Understanding the world's stories with new depth and access could create a global camaraderie that introduces new potential into our world.

A Path to Better Stories

The pandemic had many interesting consequences on journalism. We saw countless news organizations shutter and thousands of journalists struggle against the weight of the stress and anxiety of covering COVID-19 amid racial justice revolutions, climate change, the rise of authoritarianism, and more.

A shift happened in international reporting too. COVID-19 largely grounded parachute journalists. In their absence, local journalists across the world rose to prominence. Global Press, which has been publishing context-rich feature news since 2006, saw powerful influxes of audience, both directly on our platforms and via other publishers seeking out our news to serve their own audiences. Large-scale publishers like BBC, Quartz, and NPR republished stories produced by our local journalists across the world. And in our coverage countries, where many local news organizations on the ground struggled to stay afloat, free access to our stories filled their pages and offered access to important information during a difficult time.

In this early postpandemic moment, we have an extraordinary opportunity to continue this progress and chart a new way forward by choosing to move on from the parachute journalism model of the past. Let's end the extractive and reductionist narratives told by those who fundamentally lack access. The pandemic taught us that local journalists can lead the way and that they should be the reporters of record, uncovering stories that otherwise would not have been told. Whether directly or by forging new collaborations between local and global newsrooms, it is their bylines we need to be reading.

In the pages that follow, I'll lay out a path to better, more equitable, and accurate international journalism—a path that can restore trust, expand our worldview, and offer countless benefits to our beleaguered industry.

Throughout, I hope it will become powerfully clear that shifting our reliance to local journalists creates incredible opportunities for all of us to better understand each other and the world we share.

Systemic Failure

CHAPTER 1

A Broken System Delivering Bad News

Manori Wijesekera joined Global Press as a reporter in Sri Lanka in 2009. She told powerful stories about garment factories, tech innovations, land use, and women's rights. Today, more than fourteen years later, Manori runs our global training program, ensuring other local women journalists have the skills they need to claim space as professional reporters of record from dozens of communities around the world.

She has spent nearly as long as I have analyzing parachute journalism and its consequences. Unlike me, though, she has a front-row seat to the direct effects of this model, as parachute journalists swoop in to cover Sri Lanka's ongoing political and economic crises.

"I was watching Al Jazeera with some friends, and there was a white man reporting from Colombo just before the president was ousted," she told me, referring to events in the summer of 2022.

On that night, she said the reporter set up his camera in the middle of a large gathering of people he thought was a protest.

"He started his report by saying, 'People are angry. They are shouting,'" Manori recalled. "But they weren't angry. And they weren't shouting. The crowd was repeating a single word—*jayawewa*. It means, 'Victory is upon us.' The people were cheering, celebrating."

It might sound like a small detail. But it isn't. A local reporter would have understood what jayawewa meant and would have categorized the entire event differently—and more precisely.

"When I think of that coverage, I think, 'Why was this guy even here? Why do we even need him?'" Manori said. "He gave that piece to all the world, and it was totally incorrect. It left the viewer with a very biased and inaccurate perspective and understanding of Sri Lanka at that moment. And it was an important moment."

The State of Modern Journalism

I wish I could suggest that this story was unique, but I was spoiled for choice when deciding which anecdote to include here. Everywhere you look, when you know what you're looking for, prominent journalists covering international events for prestigious publications fill their reporting with unintentional errors, misunderstandings, and generalizations.

It's not because they're bad or malicious. And it's not due to fake news or misinformation. It's a lack of proximity. It's a lack of access. These misrepresentations happen when elite outsiders drop into global communities on short-term assignments.

We used to get our news about the rest of the world primarily from the bureau-based correspondent. In the later half of the twentieth century, foreign correspondents who lived in the communities they covered, often for long periods of time, brought us more consistent coverage of the world, albeit through elite outsiders' lenses. The very best foreign correspondents immersed themselves in the community, learned the language, and built a robust network of sources over many years.

One such correspondent was Carroll Bogert, now president of the acclaimed criminal justice news organization *The Marshall Project*. She was a foreign correspondent for *Newsweek* magazine in Beijing and later Moscow. She first went to China already speaking the language and later became fluent in Russian. She has a long and compelling list of incredible stories she told between 1985 and 1998 when she returned home. Atop the list was her coverage of the Tiananmen Square massacre in 1989.

"I was as close to the ground as a blonde person in Beijing could be," Bogert told me. "By that I mean I rode a bicycle, a Flying Pigeon bicycle, that was the brand every Chinese person had; I didn't have a car, and I didn't have a translator."

Her coverage of Tiananmen Square was a powerful reminder about the role foreign correspondents can play in reporting important stories from closed societies around the world.

"In the aftermath, I was in my foreign correspondent hotel, where Chinese people didn't stay. I was on deadline, and I ordered room service because I didn't have time even to leave my hotel room to go eat dinner. When the guy brought the meal, he had one of those leather folders that the bill comes in for me to sign. I opened the folder, and inside on the left-hand side, written in English, was, 'Thank you people,'" she said. "Our eyes met, and I knew that my room was bugged so we couldn't speak, but I knew what he meant. He was saying, 'Thank you for telling the world the truth about what happened to us.'"

The bureau-based correspondent was capable of telling pivotal stories in important moments like this one. The model does have some liabilities and drawbacks—namely that very few exist anymore. Over the last few decades, budget cuts have forced a majority of foreign bureaus to close, further restricting direct access to information about places in sub-Saharan Africa, Central and South America, Southeast Asia, and more. The results are unfortunate: news consumers have less direct and proximate coverage of the world today.

In a 2010 study by Dannika Lewis of Elon University, she reported that US TV networks maintained about fifteen foreign bureaus in the 1980s. But by 2007, "ABC had shut down its offices in Moscow, Paris, and Tokyo; NBC closed bureaus in Beijing, Cairo, and Johannesburg. In addition, there are no network bureaus left at all in Africa, India, or South America. Those areas together comprise about two billion people."[3] Those regions account for nearly three billion people today.

In the early 2000s, other news outlets showed a similar trend.

In 2006, for example, the Tribune Co., the corporate parent of the *Baltimore Sun*, the *Los Angeles Times*, and the *Chicago Tribune*, announced plans to shrink its international coverage by closing the foreign bureaus of the chain's smaller newspapers. At the *Baltimore Sun*, a major US daily with a one-hundred-plus-year history of operating foreign bureaus, correspondents based in Moscow and Johannesburg were reassigned to Baltimore. Their Middle East correspondent was "absorbed into the *Tribune*'s foreign network," to provide stories for all papers in the chain, according to a 2006 *Sun*

---

3   Dannika Lewis, "Foreign Correspondents in a Modern World: The Past, Present and Possible Future of Global Journalism," *The Elon Journal of Undergraduate Research in Communications 1*, no. 1, (Winter 2010), https://eloncdn.blob.core.windows.net/eu3/sites/153/2017/06/12LewisEJSpring10.pdf.

story.[4] At *Newsday*, a sister paper, bureaus in Islamabad and Beirut, the paper's last remaining bureaus, were closed by 2008.

In response to the closures, then-editor of the *Sun*, Timothy A. Franklin, announced a shift in how the paper would still cover the world: the paper would begin dispatching reporters from Baltimore on occasion.

This trend happened across major media outlets. And that's how the rise of parachute journalism began. While major newspapers initially said that international news would receive equivalent coverage this way, that hasn't been the case.

According to a LexisNexis search of the *New York Times*, the *Los Angeles Times*, and the *Boston Globe*, the number of articles that mention Africa at least twice dropped by 56 percent in the last two decades. Between 1998 and 2003, those publications produced nearly nineteen thousand articles about Africa. That number plummeted to about eighty-three hundred in the last five years.

In a world where technology allows us unlimited access to information, our ability to truly understand people and places across the world has become more limited because traditional media is no longer equipped to tell us comprehensive stories.

And the consequences are immense.

This change has limited the worldview of millions of people. It has signaled to an entire generation of news producers and consumers that the rest of the world is somehow less important.

"This is why people don't trust the media," Manori told me. "Because they can't trust the person who is telling them the story."

---

4   Nick Madigan, "Tribune Co. is closing Sun's foreign bureaus," Baltimore Sun, July 2006, accessed February 2, 2023, https://www.baltimoresun.com/news/bs-xpm-2006-07-07-0607070011-story.html.

Inadequate Options

It's important to note that individual journalists, like the Al Jazeera reporter in Manori's example, are far less at fault than the system itself. Journalists do their best to report stories accurately, but the current model makes that too difficult.

To understand the immensity of the failure that is international news today, we have to break down current coverage strategies to see how each inhibits the development of the quality reporting that news consumers require. Modern journalism predominantly uses three methods to tell international stories: parachute journalism, laptop journalism, and a skeletal bureau system.

Each of these creates unique blind spots that do a disservice to the readers, the subjects, and often the journalists themselves.

Parachute Journalism

There's something deeply romantic about parachute journalism. It's a romance I understand all too well, having dreamed of becoming one for so long. Flying into a distant country to tell important stories, doing hard-hitting interviews over the course of a few days, and putting together an article about a subject the reader in the United States would otherwise never hear about: What's not to love?

It is, of course, possible to tell important stories as a parachute journalist. But if you remove that romance, it's easy to see the immense disservice this practice can do for readers and the people at the center of the stories being told.

Few embody the modern parachute journalist more than Pulitzer Prize–winning journalist Nicholas Kristof.

Kristof has long been feted for his parachute reporting around the world. He won a Pulitzer Prize for his coverage of China and another for his coverage of Darfur. Kristof was the subject of a 2007 Ben Affleck–produced documentary, *Reporter*, and has had space on the *New York Times*'s op-ed page for more than twenty years.

For all the praise of his work, Kristof has also been the subject of significant criticism for his reporting methods.

At the root of this criticism is Kristof's victim-seeking methods. In *Reporter*, Kristof explains that he tries to find the worst and most pathetic stories in his current location. He justifies his methods by suggesting that highlighting the most devastating stories gets his readership back in the United States to care.[5]

In the film, the narrator opines that Kristof's job isn't easy because, "to quote Susan Sontag, 'Compassion is an unstable emotion.'" Later in the film, Kristof interviews a crowd of people in Democratic Republic of Congo (DRC) who were just displaced from their village due to conflict. The narrator again chimes in: "So many terrible stories. In my eyes, each warranted a column, but none of them seemed quite desperate enough for Nick."

This method is certainly not unique to Kristof. Much of his work is reminiscent of the accounts in the 1985 book by journalist Edward Behr *Anyone Here Been Raped and Speaks English?* In that book, Behr details an overheard conversation in the 1960s in DRC. In a 2006 piece for the *New York Times*, Kristof pays homage to the book:

"That was the title of a memoir by the journalist Edward Behr, and I always think of it as I go off to the Darfur region—as I'm doing right now … Although most of us don't put it so crassly, that's in a

---

5   Ben Affleck, "Reporter," New Video Group, 2008, YouTube video, https://www. youtube.com/watch?v=_mAWB8G24QQ.

sense what we're after: a victim with a wrenching tale and an ability to recount it in a way that will move readers or viewers."[6]

Kristof has long used the theory of psychic numbing, the notion that people become shut off to information when the scope of a problem becomes too large to process. "That's why I focus on an individual. I've done it over and over again," he says in the documentary.

Kristof took a brief hiatus from his column to run for governor of Oregon in 2021 before returning to the *Times* and his column. When I spoke to him in late 2022, I was curious to know if his perspective on international reporting had shifted over the years.

"I think it's fairly similar," he told me. "There is some good social science research that says people want, not exactly positivity, but they want some indication that if they pay attention to a problem, they can make it better."

As he plans to resume international travel for his columns, he says he'll continue to use his traditional recipe—"individual stories to get people to care" mixed with "larger context and also trying to show that if we were to get involved in a crisis we might actually be able to make a difference."

The parachute approach is a throwback to the 1965 study by Galtung and Ruge. If anyone is going to read about a place on the other side of the world—particularly if that place is located in Africa, South or Central Asia, or Latin America—we've been conditioned to believe the story has to be tragic enough to get their attention.

In one piece from March 2018 called "Conflict Is More Profitable Than Peace," Kristof recounted the stories he unearthed on his brief

---

6   Nicholas D. Kristof, "Anyone Here Been Raped and Speaks English?,"
     New York Times, November 2006, accessed February 2, 2023,
     https://archive.nytimes.com/kristof.blogs.nytimes.com/2006/11/08/
     anyone-here-been-raped-and-speaks-english/.

visit to Central African Republic (CAR).[7] In the article, he paints a dire picture of poverty, hunger, and desperation due to ongoing war in the country. The story opens with a mother who has lost three sons to starvation and may be losing a fourth. Kristof describes it in the opening line as "the most devastating blow any human can suffer."

Of course, none of what Kristof wrote was untrue—CAR is an extraordinarily challenging place. The fundamental flaw in the story, as with most parachute journalism, is the perspective he brought to the article. He was not writing to inform the residents of CAR about their country or the resources available to them. His goals were to get people to care and to convince the powerful in Washington, DC, to change US foreign policy.

In the article, he makes these intentions explicit when he addresses the former ambassador to the UN Nikki Haley directly: "Ambassador Haley, please understand that without peacekeeping, you're sentencing civilians to be raped and shot—and boys like Frederick Pandowan to starve."

Kristof writes in the article that he believes this is the only way anyone in the United States would pay attention—because the people of CAR are simply too different and too far away. "I realize that for many Americans, these issues seem as remote as if they unfolded on Mars," he writes, suggesting that the human beings in CAR are as unimportant to US readers as Martians.

The piece drew widespread criticism. Sarah Knuckey, a clinical professor of law who directs the Human Rights Clinic at Columbia University, called the piece "shallow" and "reckless" in an interview

---

7   Nicholas Kristof, "Conflict Is More Profitable Than Peace," New York Times, March 2018, accessed February 2, 2023, https://www.nytimes.com/2018/03/23/opinion/sunday/central-african-republic-conflict.html.

with NPR. She also took to Twitter to point out a long list of ways Kristof's piece marginalized the citizens of CAR.

"There is little recognition of the agency and work of the countless Central Africans who run NGOs, provide healthcare, work for peace, prosecute crimes, risk their lives to protect others," she wrote. She goes on to provide a list of local people, organizations, and efforts absent from the article.[8]

"A better article would highlight the many harms and challenges faced by Central Africans, elevate the many local efforts to counter the war [and] humanitarian crisis, and amplify the reforms identified as critical by local leaders," she wrote to conclude her thread.

For his part, Kristof acknowledged the criticism he received from the piece but took it in stride.

"As a journalist, we dish it out, and so we have to be prepared to take it," he said. "And the criticisms come from genuine issues that are real. Local voices often haven't gotten enough attention, so there is some validity to those points."

The absence of the local voices and the inability to seek them out all mean that even the best parachute journalists are unable to provide readers with anything more than a half portrait of the reality on the ground. Diverse sets of voices often evade parachuters because the reporters have limited context for events, limited language abilities to converse with local people, and limited access to real people.

In this case, the only CAR citizens who make the cut in Kristof's article are those who are suffering. And the only people who can do anything are people in the US government or the foreigners working in international NGOs.

---

8   Sarah Knuckey, Twitter post, March 25, 2018, 11:58 a.m., https://twitter.com/
     SarahKnuckey/status/977937807531528192.

The presentation of local people as largely helpless is interesting when you consider what's happening behind the scenes in Kristof's reporting.

"I would get nowhere if it weren't for the people I was relying on—the fixers, the interpreters," he told me.

Most parachute journalists connect with local journalists immediately upon arriving in a foreign land. Those local reporters become their "fixers," doing everything from showing them around, translating and securing interviews.

If the *Times* coverage of CAR, and other rarely covered places, was placed in the hands of these very capable local journalists, how would that change the coverage? It would certainly create room for more comprehensive depictions of the people in that country. And that could only be a good thing.

If a US newspaper article about the opioid crisis only quoted the most desperate local addicts and framed high-level leaders in another country as the only people who could save them, we'd be confused, if not outraged. If that article never quoted the local mayor or the local people running clinics we'd know it was only half told.

Perhaps the greatest weakness of parachute journalism, and really all foreign correspondence, is that they are writing these stories for audiences back home, not for the people who appear in their stories. People in CAR don't subscribe to the *New York Times*. People there speak predominantly French and Sango, a Ngbandi-based creole— not English. That also means they, generally, can't hold the publication accountable.

Kristof told me that when he goes to a place like CAR, he presumes the people in his story will not read it.

"In a lot of these countries nobody's on the internet, nobody speaks English, so I would typically presume that, no, they will not read it," he said.

I believe that Kristof meant to help the people of CAR by telling that story. He writes it in this way because he genuinely believes it is the best way to get anyone's attention—almost shaming people out of inaction.

In his conversation with me, he was kind and generous with his time, even after it was clear that our approaches to international storytelling couldn't be more different.

"I talk to university students periodically, and they often have a very strong view that Congo, for example, should be really covered by a Congolese person not by a *New York Times* reporter waltzing in," he said. "I'm all in favor of Congolese [people] writing opinion pieces and weighing in, but the larger challenge is that news organizations aren't really interested in covering Congo. And one of the few ways of getting coverage is for someone like me to bounce in."

That's true. Publishers have long lamented the lack of appetite for international news. But according to several new studies, including one by Global Press in partnership with Goodwin Simon Strategic Research and Wonder: Strategies for Good, which was published in 2023, that view may be outdated. Our report showed there was significant demand among large sections of the US population for higher-quality international news. And a majority said hearing more from local journalists was a key way international coverage could improve.[9] More on this later.

---

9   Lexmi Parthasarathy and Cristi Hegranes, "Unlocking U.S. Audience Demand for International News," Media Impact Funders, February 2023, accessed February 31, 2023, https://bit.ly/globalpressaudience.

None of this is to say there's no place for parachute journalism. But there are ways to provide more equitable and accurate stories that do not undermine the dignity and reality of the people parachute journalism covers while reinforcing deeply ingrained stereotypes.

Too many stories start with the assumptions that African states are doomed to fail and that people across the continent are victims incapable of any agency, allergic to success. Greater contexts on the history of colonialism or recent progress are ignored because they don't fit the simple narrative, and readers are given no credit for the ability to understand nuance.

Combine that lens with the limited amount of time the journalist has in a place, their limited experience of the local culture, language issues, and limited access to sources, and such stories are systematically incapable of providing the accurate reporting those in the story deserve and the reader needs.

Laptop Journalism

Next time you're reading a piece on an international event, check the dateline to see where it was reported. The location name should be in all caps at the start of an article. You may be surprised to discover that the story was reported thousands of miles, several countries or even an ocean away.

The journalist on the byline hasn't discovered teleportation. They most likely researched and wrote the story from their desk. This is laptop journalism—often the least expensive international journalism option (save for stories cobbled together through artificial intelligence, which shouldn't count as journalism at all).

Sometimes an international piece won't have a dateline at all. This typically indicates that no original reporting was done, and sources and information were merely scraped from press releases, Twitter posts, or previously published stories.

Laptop journalism isn't just for small, online outfits that lack real reporters anymore. This practice is common at large legacy outlets too.

Stories in the *Washington Post* that originate in Africa might be filed in Washington, DC. Telling a story from across an ocean is obviously a problem, but often, the distance between events and reporting is less clear to readers. Sometimes, a story about the continent doesn't include any original reporting at all.

In one story from July 2022, the *Post* ran a story under the headline "Climate Change Is Killing More Elephants Than Poaching, Kenyan Officials Say."[10] The piece features quotes from a previously published BBC piece, data from a previously published Reuters story and online government press releases. No local voices at all.

Think about laptop reporting like this: If you were tasked with writing a story about a plane crash in rural Alaska from Miami, how could you possibly do it thoroughly or accurately? If you had no contacts in Alaska, how could you get beyond a surface level understanding of events?

So when an intern at the *Post* files a story from DC about a plane crash in Mogadishu, it should be cause for concern. A laptop journalist, no matter how skilled a writer, will inevitably struggle to tell a complete and accurate story because they lack total proximity and access.

For many, including former foreign correspondent Howard French, the reliance on laptop reporting is concerning.

---

10   Jennifer Hassan, "Climate Change Is Killing More Elephants Than Poaching, Kenyan Officials Say," Washington Post, July 2022, accessed February 2, 2023, https://www. washingtonpost.com/world/2022/07/28/kenya-elephants-drought-climate-change/.

"This proliferating model of little travel and calling things in from Dakar for all of West Africa is the worst. Let's call it what it is: Africa coverage on the cheap," French tweeted in June of 2022 in response to the *Post*'s coverage of events in Nigeria reported from Senegal, where they have a full-time correspondent.[11]

French went on to say that the remote coverage was due to "a lack of commitment" to coverage from Africa "from big US media companies." When one follower asked: "Aren't there Nigerian reporters who could file these stories?" French responded, "There certainly are."

We'd see the problems with international laptop journalism more quickly if we expected local people across Africa to have a voice in their own stories. But we've been conditioned to their invisibility, so laptop journalism rarely raises any flags.

Like parachute journalism, I'm not suggesting that this practice has no place in journalism. After all, during breaking news, a laptop reporter getting the basic facts is often all that's possible and all that's required. When an earthquake happens in Indonesia or a bomb goes off in Kenya, a journalist's first duty is to inform readers of the main event as soon as possible. A laptop journalist can do that.

The problem is that many of those stories aren't ever supplemented or followed up with thorough, accurate reporting.

Scaled-Back Bureaus

That brings us back to bureaus, and the hole their loss has left in international journalism. There were, of course, problems with this model too. Bureau-based correspondents are almost, by definition, elite.

"How do you get to be a foreign correspondent? Privilege," Bogert, the former foreign correspondent for *Newsweek*, told me. "My

---

11   Howard French, Twitter post, June 7, 2022, 10:26 a.m., https://twitter.com/hofrench/status/1534177595591360513.

parents took me abroad for the first time when I was a child. I went to good schools where I was able to study obscure languages. Foreign correspondents were, in my day, and still are, almost universally white and extremely male."

The other fundamental tension with this model is that foreign correspondents, no matter how immersed in the community, are focused on telling stories for their home audience, often relegating local people as a means to an end. And when journalism is about people that it isn't for, the same accountability problems we've already encountered will once again arise.

"I did feel sometimes that I would just as soon not have the local population read what I was writing," Bogert told me. "I knew that I was objectifying them or turning them into something that would be comprehensible to my readers back home. In foreign correspondence you're always writing something that reduces somebody's very, very complex experience to a few sentences. Who I was talking to was so different from who I was writing about."

Bogert recalled one of the few times she came face-to-face with a local person who was unhappy with how he was portrayed in a *Newsweek* story, or rather, on its cover.

The story was about new, private entrepreneurs being allowed to operate in Moscow. "We did a cover story about these two young entrepreneurs, and the picture was of a young guy who was on the Arbat, the big shopping street, selling stuff," she said. "Somehow he found his way to the *Newsweek* office and said 'What was my picture doing on the cover of *Newsweek* magazine? I could get in trouble.'"

Bogert says, in hindsight, he was right.

"Did we sufficiently think about that? No, we didn't. That's the nightmare of the foreign correspondent—that you write something about somebody that really harms them. Can I say for sure that nobody was ever harmed by my journalism? I cannot."

For all its limitations, though, the bureau model had a lot to recommend it. Unfortunately, the only locations that continue to benefit from it are the already well-covered centers of power.

Where once there might have been a bureau, now the only way to cover the news is through a laptop or a parachute.

Who's Left to Tell Accurate Stories?

This is the landscape for international news coverage. What is clearly missing is a strategy for reporting that emphasizes accuracy and proximity. While parachute journalism can offer drama, laptop journalism provides speed, and bureaus in a few capitals can tell stories in traditional areas of power, the events occurring in most of the world rarely receive thorough, long-term, comprehensive coverage.

And that means even invested international news readers struggle to understand context for the majority of communities around the world. The stories they hear from entire continents are one-note and shallow—and often sensationalized.

CHAPTER 2

Sensationalism over Accuracy

News needs to be compelling. Whatever the story, every journalist knows to seek the perspective that will most grip the reader and keep them reading paragraph after paragraph or watching minute after minute. But in international news, it has become far too common for news outlets to push beyond captivating language, images, and video and let assumptions drag us into a realm that is disturbingly close to fiction.

Take, for instance, CNN's coverage of a 7.4 magnitude earthquake in Nepal in 2015. Nepal is a country that doesn't experience earthquakes very often, and its infrastructure couldn't handle the shock. The results were predictably devastating, and so, following the 1965 *Structure of Foreign News* standard, Nepal became newsworthy at least for that day and the chaotic weeks that followed.

To tell this story, CNN sent one of its stars, Dr. Sanjay Gupta. Gupta had developed a very compelling model of coverage for such events. Being a trained neurosurgeon, he would visit a disaster zone, report on the damage, and then somehow at some point in the story, cross the line between doctor and journalist and attempt to save someone's life.

This made for very compelling television. The viewer could learn about some horror abroad and watch as Gupta became embroiled in a dramatic set of circumstances that required him to step into the operating theater—all recorded on camera.

Before Nepal, he'd already used this technique in Iraq and Haiti.

Unsurprisingly, Gupta's trip to Kathmandu was no different. When he arrived at Bir Hospital, the country's largest public hospital, it was, of course, completely overwhelmed. Gupta's coverage on CNN detailed how he scrubbed in and performed brain surgery on an adorable eight-year-old girl named Salina Dahal.

"Salina will live," Gupta triumphantly told the camera.

It was a perfect story. In fact, it was a little too perfect to be true. Gupta undeniably did perform brain surgery on someone, and he did save that person's life.

But CNN's own coverage suggested it was impossible that that someone was eight-year-old Salina.

On the day of the surgery, Gupta's producer, Tim Hume, published a story online that mentioned Salina. In that story, a picture of Salina showed that she had minor injuries. (Her medical records would later confirm that she had suffered minor head wounds and a broken wrist.) Hume's story stated that she was one of the lucky ones who would make a full recovery.

Why, then, was she Gupta's brain surgery patient in the TV story just a few hours later?

Such an inconsistency would likely have gone unnoticed, if not for the fact one of our local Nepalese journalists, Shilu Manandhar, received a tip: the girl on CNN was not the girl who had the operation.[12]

Shilu began to investigate.

Closer examination of the footage by medical experts confirmed that the heart rate shown on the screen would be inconsistent with that of a small child. So who was Gupta operating on? And what happened to Salina?

Shilu did what any local journalist would do: she started looking for Salina. In the immediate aftermath of the earthquake that was no easy task. Roads were still closed, and transportation was limited. The CNN coverage had misspelled Salina's last name and the name of the village where she came from.

"I had a very difficult time finding her," Shilu recalled.

With the help of sources at local police stations, health clinics, and a local journalist who had taken photographs of patients at Bir Hospital in hopes of reuniting families, she found an image of Salina holding the same teddy bear she'd had on CNN.

Over the course of many weeks, Shilu meticulously got to the bottom of what happened.

"I went knocking on doors," she said. "I went back to the village where I thought she was from and spoke to local people. These villages are very small; everybody knows each other."

And then Shilu found her. The first thing Shilu did was look at Salina's head—no evidence of brain surgery.

Shilu spoke to Salina's grandfather who confirmed Shilu's suspicions. Salina had not had brain surgery. Shilu also confirmed that no

---

12   Shilu Manandhar, "CNN Falsely Claims Dr. Sanjay Gupta Performed Brain Surgery on 8-Year-Old after Earthquake in Nepal," Global Press Journal, July 2015, accessed March 6, 2023, https://globalpressjournal.com/asia/nepal/cnn-falsely-claims-dr-sanjay-gupta-performed-brain-surgery-on-8-year-old-quake-victim-in-nepal/.

one had asked permission to put footage of Salina's on television or her picture on the CNN website.

But the mystery wasn't yet solved. If Salina wasn't the one who had brain surgery, as Gupta declared on TV, who did? Shilu even began to wonder if Gupta had operated on anyone at all.

Request for comment from CNN went unanswered at first. But as our story grew, CNN's director of public relations, Neel Khairzada, eventually sent us unseen, embargoed footage of Gupta in an operating room, using a handsaw on someone's head. That proved the operation was real. But that was the limit of the network's helpfulness. CNN refused us access to talk to Gupta, so our on-the-ground investigation kept going.

Eventually, Shilu found the teenage girl who had brain surgery that day in the aftermath of the earthquake. Her name is Sandhya Chalise, a fourteen-year-old, whose injuries were severe. When Shilu found her, the evidence of the surgery was plain—shaved head and a long scar. Her mother confirmed that she'd had surgery and the doctors at Bir Hospital had saved her life.

When Shilu asked about the CNN doctor and camera crew, Sandhya's mother didn't know what she was talking about. No one had told her that an American journalist-doctor had performed part of the operation. No one had asked her permission to film the surgery either.

Reporting any story in the aftermath of a disaster is chaotic, and mistakes can happen. But this was an unusual case, in part because CNN got the story right before they got it wrong.

Remember that CNN online article that described Salina as one of the lucky ones with just minor injuries? That article also correctly identified Sandhya Chalise as Gupta's brain surgery patient. But that version of the story was deleted and replaced about nine hours after it was first published.

In the new version, any mention of Sandhya had been scrubbed. And to match with the television segment, in the new version, Salina was now Gupta's patient.

Portions of the story, including sentences that originally described Sandhya's injuries—blood clots in her brain—were used, word for word, to describe Salina. The story's original lines about Salina, which correctly described her minor injuries, were deleted.

Concerningly, the article didn't include any mention of having been updated, as is common for all news organizations. We only found this version in the course of our investigation by using the Wayback Machine, an internet archiving tool. That's how we found Sandhya and proved that CNN had knowingly swapped the girls.

CNN continued to refuse to let us speak to Gupta and offered only minimal comments. So Global Press turned to longtime NPR media reporter David Folkenflik for advice. Folkenflik reviewed all of our materials and agreed to do a story of his own. When he reached out to CNN, he was quickly connected to Gupta.

Finally, pinned down by facts, CNN released a statement:

"Journalism is not brain surgery. But brain surgery is brain surgery. We are so proud that Sanjay was one of the few reporters in Nepal to cover the earthquake, and while there, was asked to help save a young victim's life. As we reported, he assisted the surgeons at Bir Hospital by performing a craniotomy on a young victim. Some reporting has suggested it was not the young girl we, at the time of our own reporting in the midst of the crisis, believed her to be. We will try to verify that. Regardless, Sanjay spent a week in Nepal, helped to save a young life in the operating room, and we couldn't be prouder of him. He has our full and unequivocal support."[13]

A week later, CNN issued a correction. And Gupta appeared on CNN's morning show *New Day* with Chris Cuomo to explain what had happened. To his credit, Gupta took responsibility for the error, saying he was the one who said the girl's name should be changed.

(Neel Khairzada, Sanjay Gupta, and two of Gupta's former producers did not respond to invitations to speak on the subject for this book.)

In a 2022 interview, Folkenflik reflected on the story and the complex set of events.

"I like to pull back the veil and understand how major journalistic players, in newsworthy moments, make news judgments that affect how we view the world," he said. "That's part of my remit."

Folkenflik had covered Gupta's previous stories where he crossed the line from journalist to doctor. "I wrote about this when he and Anderson Cooper went down to Haiti," he recalled. "It's a tension. Off the air you will find executives for various networks saying this stuff helps pay the bills, and it helps people pay attention to the things they need to pay attention to and might not otherwise."

Do the ends justify the means? Folkenflik isn't sure.

"The question is, is this poverty porn, disaster porn? And that's a real issue for these outlets to acknowledge and wrestle with," he said.

On the Precipice of Entertainment

Perhaps it was all an honest mistake. Or perhaps Gupta and Hume chose the local person they thought most likely to arouse sympathy—

---

13   Brian Stelter, "CNN's Sanjay Gupta Clarifies Reporting Following Nepal Earthquake," July 2015, accessed February 2, 2023, https://money.cnn.com/2015/07/08/media/sanjay-gupta/.

the adorable eight-year-old with the teddy bear. Perhaps they felt she was their best hope of getting eyes on the crisis in Nepal. If that was their calculus, they probably weren't wrong.

But that doesn't excuse the tactics that were employed. It doesn't excuse the blatant switching of identities, the lack of transparent updating of their site, nor does it excuse the lack of permission requested or obtained by CNN from either of the girls who were featured in a story that was viewed by millions.

A renowned and award-winning journalist in her own right, Shilu says this was not her favorite story to cover. She had no interest in the limelight or barrage of media attention that followed her reporting, both locally and globally. She says she reported on the story for a simple reason—dignity.

"I pursued the story because theirs was inaccurate. It was disrespectful. These girls deserve dignity, and the readers deserve transparency. It was important to set the record straight," she said.

And she's right. These tactics would never be employed in a story that took place in Kansas instead of Kathmandu. And if they were, the consequences would be swift and severe.

Shilu's editor on the story was the news director at that time, Krista Karch.

"This little girl and her family didn't have a television, had no knowledge whatsoever that video of Salina had been broadcast worldwide. Pictures of her were on Shutterstock. For a while, she had an IMDB page. I would be outraged if those things happened to any of my children, and would do anything I could to ensure that CNN faced consequences," Krista wrote to me in a 2023 email. "But Salina's family had zero resources to do that."

Unfortunately, the media's obsession with war-poverty-disaster-disease narratives means that people like Salina and Sandhya are often made into dramatic characters instead of real individuals. Local people are depicted as hopeless, hapless, and lacking so much agency that they don't even warrant asking for their permission before putting their injured children on television for the world to see. Ultimately, it seems, local people must serve as part of the entertainment, or else, they're of little value to news organizations.

The consequences of this narrative sensationalism are many. First, it means we only hear about stories from Nepal on Nepal's worst day. The parachute model guarantees that the coverage will end when the drama dies down. But perhaps more disturbingly, it reinforces a dangerously outdated worldview—one in which the "Westerners" are the narrators and the heroes. Local people are there only for our pity and maybe, if they're lucky, our brief attention and small donations.

It would take Kathmandu years to recover, but as far as news organizations like CNN were concerned, the story ended as the dramatic footage turned into a rebuilding effort.

And that creates a distorted sense of what is really going on in the world around us.

Distorted Reality

The distortion of international news comes largely from the old standards we've inherited from decades past. According to these standards, stories about anywhere outside of a few major metropolises must always be negative, dramatic, and victim-centered.

And that creates a distorted picture of life around the world. The earthquake in Nepal was undeniably newsworthy, but because few other stories from Nepal ever reach mass audiences, it's easy to be left with the impression that Nepal is a hopeless place defined by disaster.

And nothing could be further from the truth.

Many of the major events occurring in countries that are usually bound by *Structure of Foreign News* rules aren't about warlords or starvation, they're about hope, innovation, and human potential. Some of the top tech startups are being founded in Africa. Some of the most innovative ways to take on climate change are being explored on the coast of the Indian Ocean. And stories of resistance against draconian oppression of women aren't just coming from Texas; they're coming from Mongolia.

Essentially, if the media only endeavors to tell the most dramatic stories that happen outside our borders, we will always get the sensational over the accurate.

In a class I teach at Georgetown, Explorations of Equity in Global Journalism, I pair students up for what seems like a pretty typical profile writing exercise. But there's a catch—the interviewer must exclusively ask questions about negative aspects of the person's past and personality. The assignment is uncomfortable. Students divulge small stories about embarrassing moments and bad experiences.

Once the assignment is done, students have a clearer idea of the flaws of the disaster-driven approach to news reporting that pins people and places to a single story. When asked, no student said the information they shared was wholly accurate. They left out the most sensitive parts, offering only half truths and limited details. And no matter what stories they shared, no one felt those revelations summed them up entirely. In the end, one thing was very clear to everyone in the room: one horrible event or mistake does not represent the totality of who an individual is.

To wrap up the assignment we all watched the 2009 TED Talk by Nigerian writer Chimamanda Ngozi Adichie, in which she put into words the dangers of a single story. And it has direct application to international journalism:

"It is impossible to talk about the single story without talking about power. There is a word, an Igbo word, that I think about whenever I think about the power structures of the world, and it is 'nkali.' It's a noun that loosely translates to 'to be greater than another.' Like our economic and political worlds, stories too are defined by the principle of nkali. How they are told, who tells them, when they're told, how many stories are told, are really dependent on power. Power is the ability not just to tell the story of another person, but to make it the definitive story of that person."[14]

No one's story can be summed up entirely by their worst day—and that's as true for people in Nepal as it is about my students.

The Price of a Good Story at All Costs

I've been told many times that the economics of journalism require scaled-back international coverage and juiced up stories.

But these strategies do real harm to the people being covered and to the consumers of the news. In the first place, the people in these stories find their lives misrepresented and their experiences glossed over. Those who read or view the news may find themselves entertained, but they are not particularly well informed. Both cause people to lose trust in the news.

In the years since the Nepal earthquake, Shilu has become one of the most prominent journalists in Nepal. She has covered earthquake recovery for years. And in 2018, she led a major investigation into fraud and misuse of international aid for the country's postearthquake recovery.

---

14 Chimamanda Ngozi Adichie, "The Danger of a Single Story," TED, 2009, YouTube video, https://www.youtube.com/watch?v=D9lhs241zeg.

For his part, Gupta was the subject of minor, short-term criticism for his actions in Nepal. He remains a prominent figure on CNN, though a search of CNN's archives suggests that the last time he performed an operation for the camera was in Nepal in 2015.

The reality of our world today requires us to understand people and places more completely. And to do that we need storytellers who can help us understand that the world is more than disaster and starvation. We need reporters with access to stories about innovation, technology, and progress.

If news is meant to provide clarity and understanding to its consumers, we must tell more of these stories. To do otherwise is a disservice to our readers and viewers—and to ourselves as journalists.

CHAPTER 3

Too Much Risk,
Not Enough Care

The current model for producing international news isn't just a problem because it fails to capture stories accurately. This model is also putting the people at the center of the industry—journalists—into high-risk situations without adequate support. We are often quick to lament the poor quality of journalism in the world today, but we rarely acknowledge the parallel problem that most journalism jobs offer low quality employment.

Nothing has illustrated this quite like the treatment journalists received during the pandemic. When COVID-19 reached pandemic status, journalists were at risk the same way other frontline workers like EMTs, factory workers, and grocery clerks were, yet their employers provided extremely limited support to protect their physical and mental health.

Seeing journalists as frontline workers felt unnatural to many. Journalists are usually lumped in with the professional classes. But while most professionals could work from home during the pandemic, journalists were out in the field. Undeniably, their work was essential. Without journalists, information about a disease that was killing thousands a day would have been hard to access and share quickly.

At times, journalists were central to sharing accurate information while government experts lagged behind. It was common knowledge that COVID-19 was an airborne disease before the Centers for Disease Control and Prevention admitted it—because of news.

Despite the fact that journalists were frontline workers sharing life-saving information, 30 percent of news organizations did not supply a single piece of protective equipment to their journalists in the field, according to the Journalism and the Pandemic Project.[15] A joint effort from the International Center for Journalists and the Tow Center for Digital Journalism at Columbia University, the project studied the impacts on the field worldwide.

The project further found that negligence went beyond ignoring risks to the physical health of journalists. In the same global survey, 69 percent of journalists rated the psychological and emotional impacts of dealing with the COVID-19 crisis as the most difficult aspect of their work during the period.

Those psychological impacts can't be overstated. About one-third of reporters surveyed by the Dart Center for Journalism and Trauma between September 2021 and February 2022 reported symptoms that Elana Newman, PhD, the research director at the Dart Center, said were consistent with a PTSD diagnosis.[16]

---

15   International Center for Journalists, "New Global Survey Raises Red Flags for Journalism in the COVID-19 Era," ICFJ, October 2020, accessed February 2, 2023, https://www.icfj.org/news/new-global-survey-raises-red-flags-journalism-covid-19-era.

16   River Smith, Elana Newman, Susan Drevo, and Autumn Slaughter, "Covering Trauma: Impact on Journalists," Dart Center for Journalism & Trauma, July 2015, accessed February 2, 2023, https://dartcenter.org/content/covering-trauma-impact-on-journalists.

Now, a few years out from the worst of it, many more studies are popping up, confirming what journalists in the field already knew: covering a mass casualty event that lasted for years had deep and lasting psychological consequences for the people telling the stories. Across the industry Slack support groups popped up; some journalists took breaks, making brave and public announcements that they were not OK. But the response from news organizations was typically muted.

"I'm so sick of the 'This is the job, choke it down and get back out there' mentality," a friend who works at a major DC-based publication told me in the weeks leading up to her decision to quit.

Often, the rationale for this lack of care is either economics or a reliance on the old trope that my friend was referring to—the one that says journalists are risk-loving people constantly on the lookout for a burning building to run into. This reckless stereotype not only excuses news outlets from providing services and care, but it also discourages journalists from reporting risk or even trauma for fear they won't get the next big assignment.

That fear is well founded. In the current journalism model, there's very limited job security for even the best reporters. The *New York Times* reported that an estimated thirty-seven thousand reporters were laid off in the first year of the pandemic.[17] And this was despite the fact that audience demand for news was surging.

A 2021 study by comScore, a media measurement company, found that the number of minutes spent by readers at news sites increased 46 percent from March 2020 to April 2021.[18] And overall visits shot up 57 percent among US-based news sites. Similarly, a 2020 study by GlobalWebIndex, an audience research company, found that

---

17   Marc Tracy, "News Media Outlets Have Been Ravaged by the Pandemic," New
      York Times, April 2020, accessed February 2, 2023, https://www.nytimes.
      com/2020/04/10/business/media/news-media-coronavirus-jobs.html.

18   Ibid.

in response to the pandemic and the lockdown, 49 percent of US consumers and 39 percent of UK consumers were reading more news stories on social media.[19]

While putting their lives on the line, journalists saw their salaries cut and their colleagues laid off, all while demand for their work was sky high.

Outside the United States, the situation was even worse. Many journalists around the world faced all the same risks, plus an additional crisis. In some countries, journalists were not considered essential frontline workers, and their forced quarantine became an excuse for a direct assault on press freedom and access to information.

In Uganda, for example, the situation was dire. Just as the pandemic strained governments and businesses, it also decimated the newspapers that covered them. Thanks to plummeting newsstand sales, about half of the country's roughly fifty print outlets shut down, at least temporarily, according to the African Centre for Media Excellence.[20]

By 2021, shuttered papers in Uganda included three local-language dailies—*Orumuri*, *Etop*, and *Rupiny*—that were the sole print news sources for their communities. Even prominent English-language papers, such as *New Vision* and the *Daily Monitor*, suffered cuts.[21] For other publications, printing the paper at all became impossible, so they resorted to being online only. Because less than a quarter

---

19   Global Web Index, "Coronavirus Research: March 2020, Release 3: Multi-market research," globalwebindex.com, accessed February 2, 2023. https://www.gwi.com/hubfs/1.%20Coronavirus%20Research%20PDFs/GWI%20coronavirus%20findings%20March%202020%20-%20Multi-Market%20data%20(Release%203).pdf.

20   Apophia Agiresaasi, "Coronavirus Claims an Unexpected Victim: Newspapers," Global Press Journal, January 2021, accessed February 2, 2023, https://globalpress-journal.com/africa/uganda/coronavirus-claims-unexpected-victim-newspapers/.

21   Ibid.

of Ugandans use the internet, that meant fewer people had access to news during an election season.

Newspaper editors across Kampala told Apophia Agiresaasi, a Global Press reporter in Uganda who covered the media during the pandemic, that staff shortages and budget cuts made it difficult to scrutinize the government's pandemic response and elections. An editor at the *Observer*, a major daily paper, told her that he couldn't assign a reporter to each of the eleven presidential candidates, as he had done previously.[22] When contenders Bobi Wine and Patrick Amuriat were arrested because their events allegedly violated coronavirus crowd restrictions, he didn't have enough journalists to report on the full gamut of uprisings.

His understaffed team also faced significant security risks. His remaining staffers sometimes had to file under the byline "By Our Reporter" to protect them from retribution when they interviewed demonstrators.

All this was happening while the world needed good journalism more than ever. Our industry now has fewer journalists facing ever more serious crises and escalating risks both here and abroad.

The Reality for Journalists

The difficulties journalists face didn't start with the pandemic—the pandemic simply emphasized and exacerbated long-standing norms in the industry.

Journalism has always been a risky profession. But now, the risks out in the field have been supplemented by the anxiety of being a working journalist at all. This has long been an industry that chroni-

---

22   Ibid.

cally underpays its talent. It offers a career path in which few ever receive reasonable benefits and job security.

For those who hoped the worst of the pandemic job losses happened in 2020 and 2021, 2022 offered no respite. Hundreds were laid off at CNN and Gannett, a hiring freeze and layoffs at NPR, and even the *Washington Post* cut its well-regarded Sunday magazine in the last few months of the year.[23]

The precarity of employment often motivates journalists to take greater risks with little to no support from employers to cover insurance or legal needs. Many are forced to work freelance, with no access to benefits at all. Others leave the profession altogether, a threat to audiences in need of accurate information in this complex global moment.

For those who do get jobs in journalism today, pay is low. A journalist with five years of experience can expect to earn less than $65,000 in most of the United States.[24] Around the world, it's worse. Journalists are often so underemployed they are forced to resort to "brown envelope" journalism—accepting bribes to cover stories favorably—because salaries are too low to survive.

If you can get a job and accept the low salary and lack of benefits, there are other difficulties ahead. To make up for limited staff, each journalist is now expected to cover far more than they would have a generation ago. A journalist focused on international stories today might be expected to show expertise across an entire continent, rather than a city.

---

23   Charlotte Klein, "Layoffs and Hiring Freezes: Media Industry Ends 2022 With Bad News for Journalists," Vanity Fair, December 2022, accessed February 2, 2023, https://www.vanityfair.com/news/2022/12/layoffs-and-hiring-freezes-media-industry-ends-2022-with-bad-news-for-journalists.

24   Matthew Ingram, "Everyone Is Admitting What They Get Paid to Work in Journalism," Columbia Journalism Review, Novemeber 2019, accessed February 2, 2023, https://www.cjr.org/cjr_outbox/google-doc-journalism-media-pay.php.

It's more work and more responsibility with ever-declining incentives. Considering the risks, it's amazing anyone still wants to pursue this career at all.

Insecure and Unsupported

Given the state of employment in the industry, it's hardly surprising that little care is taken over the security of the individual journalist—particularly if you have a holistic definition of security.

Across our industry, there is no security parity between foreign correspondents and local journalists. A foreigner, for example, likely has a wealth of insurance, from kidnap and ransom to medevac coverage. They have drivers and flak jackets and helmets and translators and passports—the good kind that get you out of a country quickly.

None of these tools are typically offered to local reporters or fixers, who often work for day rates without contracts or any form of protection. Global insurance companies deny coverage for reporters in places like Sudan and Zimbabwe, and major news outlets rarely offer local reporters gear, drivers, or safety resources should things go bad.

The consequences of this lack of care are immense. To see this, we need look no farther than south of the US border.

Mexico is where Global Press launched its first news bureau in 2006, and it is widely considered to be the most dangerous place in the world for journalists. In 2022, nineteen journalists were murdered for their work and a Mexican journalist was attacked every fourteen hours. Between 2000 and 2022, more than 150 reporters were killed there. Thousands more were harassed and intimidated.[25]

In 2019, broadcast journalist Monserrat Ortiz says she began receiving threats on her personal Facebook account after her investigation into a man with a history of violence against former girlfriends.[26] She told Global Press reporters Mar Garcia and Avigaí Silva that she enrolled in Mexico's federal Mechanism for the Protection of Defenders of Human Rights and Journalists, but leadership in the organization did little to reassure her. Created in 2012 and attached to the interior ministry, the mechanism provides camera systems, panic buttons, police protection, and other assistance to those at risk. But the system is known to be overburdened, underfunded, and understaffed, with just forty-five employees for nearly fifteen hundred beneficiaries.

"They give you a panic button," Ortiz told Global Press. "I promise you that if some hitman is going to kill me, they're not going to wait for me to activate my panic button and a patrol car to show up fifteen minutes later before they do so." At least seven journalists were murdered while under state protection between 2011 and 2020, according to government data.[27]

Over that same time period, according to the LatAm Journalism Review, a project of the Knight Center, journalism has been one of the five lowest salaried professions in Mexico.[28]

25 Mar García and Avigaí Silva, "Mexican Journalists Confront Physical Threats and Economic Turmoil," Global Press Journal, December 2022, accessed February 2, 2023, https://globalpressjournal.com/americas/mexico/mexican-journalists-confront-physical-threats-economic-turmoil/.

26 Ibid.

27 Ibid.

28 Janelle Matous, "Salary for Journalists in Mexico among the 5 Lowest in the Country, Survey Finds," LatAm Journalism Review, April 2014, accessed February 2, 2023, https://latamjournalismreview.org/articles/salary-for-journalists-in-mexico-among-the-5-lowest-in-the-country-survey-finds/.

This pattern repeats itself across the world. Local journalists face far greater risk of intimidation, injury, and death for far less compensation or care. There are, of course, times when a parachute journalist is able to tell a story that local reporters can't for security reasons. And then there are the times when foreign correspondents die too. We know the names Daniel Pearl and Jamal Khashoggi—and rightfully so. They were martyrs to the power and importance of journalism, and they deserve remembrance. But far less publicized are all the local journalists who have died for the coverage they provided. According to the Committee to Protect Journalists, 88 percent of the journalists who have been killed since 1992 were local journalists.[29] They deserve the same honor. And their living colleagues deserve the respect and protections we offer to US and European correspondents.

Death isn't the only punishment for local journalists who dare to tell true stories about their communities. In 2017, in Myanmar, the local journalists Wa Lone and Kyaw Soe Oo were arrested for helping international Reuters journalists investigate the deaths of ten Rohingya Muslim boys. After the story was published, Lone and Oo were arrested and imprisoned—where they stayed for more than five hundred days. Even when their story won the Pulitzer Prize, they remained condemned to their seven-year sentences—until they were freed after their lawyer, Amal Clooney, helped them secure presidential amnesty in 2019.[30]

---

29   Committee to Protect Journalists, "Database of Attacks on the Press 1992–Present," cpj.com, accessed February 2, 2023, https://cpj.org/data/.

30   Reuters Media Center, "Remarks from Amal Clooney, Barrister and Counsel to Reuters, Wa Lone and Kyaw Soe Oo at CPJ's 'Press Behind Bars: Undermining Justice and Democracy' event at U.N.," Reuters, September 2018, accessed February 2, 2023, https://www.reuters.com/article/rpb-amalclooneycpj/remarks-from-amal-clooney-barrister-and-counsel-to-reuters-wa-lone-and-kyaw-soe-oo-at-cpjs-press-behind-bars-undermining-justice-and-democracy-event-at-u-n-idUSKCN1M82LF.

All of this is to say that the violence local journalists face in Mexico, Myanmar, and many other countries is often far more extreme than their counterparts in the United States or Europe. And far from reducing these risks, the current model of international coverage often increases them.

For Bobby Ghosh, an acclaimed foreign correspondent who was the longest serving print journalist in Iraq while working for *TIME* magazine, the disparity between his security and that of the local journalists he worked closely with was difficult to square.

"I was always aware that I could, at any moment, get on a plane and leave and there would be no cost to myself and very little cost to my career. Nobody would hold it against me," he told me. "But the local reporters who were helping me, or with whom I was working, simply did not have that luxury. They could not escape. They were navigating far more difficult terrain, even though we were traveling in the same place at the same time."

Ghosh says that local journalists carry unfathomable additional pressure, from mental and psychological pressure to social pressure and fear for their neighbors and family members.

"There's this awareness that if they said the wrong thing, if they did the wrong thing, then their loved ones would be at risk," he said. "What's worse, if I said the wrong thing or wrote the wrong things, they would be the ones at the pointy end of the spear. Even long after I had left, they would still be reaping what I had sown."

He's right. Translators, fixers, and drivers are commonly harassed, arrested, or even killed after the foreign journalist leaves the country.

The lack of parity between foreign and local reporters doesn't end there. Not only do these local reporters put their safety on the line, but they are also often asked to put aside their own journalistic credentials or ambitions and do most of the work on a piece while receiving little or none of the credit. When they're paid to be fixers, they find the sources; they ask the questions; they translate the answers; they set up the photo shoot; and they book the government interviews—all so a parachute journalist can write it up, get credit, and receive far better pay.

For Indian journalist Priyanka Borpujari, this indignity is all too familiar. In 2019, she wrote a piece for the *Columbia Journalism Review* (*CJR*) in which she detailed the experiences of Indian journalists relegated to being fixers.[31]

Borpujari describes one incident involving Neha Dixit, an investigative journalist with a fifteen-year track record who was contacted by a professor at Northwestern University. Dixit received an email with the subject line: "Fixer needed." In the body of the email, the professor explained: "My colleagues and I are working on a story about illegal organ trafficking in India and are in need of sources for the story. We were wondering if you could help us with finding sources and guiding us around Delhi?"

This was hardly unusual for Dixit, despite the fact that she was the recipient of the Chameli Devi Jain Award—the highest honor given to women journalists in India.

"Why not hire Dixit as a reporter, rather than as a fixer, which would likely lead to a better understanding of India's complex realities?" Borpujari asked in her article. And I echo the question. Why are the local reporters, the ones with the context and the access—and the ones who front the majority of the risk—the ones who don't receive the bylines, the credit, or the security?

This is offensive not just because it sidelines the people doing most of the work. It also puts the best journalists in a location—the

---

31 Priyanka Borpujari, "The Problem with 'Fixers,'" Columbia Journalism Review, Summer 2019, accessed February 2, 2023, https://www.cjr.org/special_report/fixers.php.

journalists that the local population relies upon for trustworthy news that they consume—into significant danger.

When the Cost Is Too High

When we think about journalist security, physical attacks and detention most often come to mind. But it's actually the interconnected assault of threats across physical, emotional, digital, and legal security fronts that makes the profession unbearable at times. And when we expand security to include these ideas, we find that news organizations fare even poorer.

A physical security emergency, like a mugging or assault, can quickly become a digital security emergency if a laptop or cell phone is stolen in the process. A digital security emergency, like online trolling, can have significant emotional security and even job security consequences.

Too often news organizations offer a bit of up-front training, like Hostile Environment and First Aid Training (HEFAT) and then rely on crisis response in the event something goes wrong. In my experience, HEFAT training actually increases stress and anxiety rather than alleviating it. And crisis response tends to focus on legal and reputational risks rather than journalist security and well-being.

According to the International Women's Media Foundation, as many as 70 percent of women journalists have reported experiencing digital harassment.[32] It's a top driver of women leaving the field.

All of this should fall under the responsibility of publishers, but too many do not take a holistic view of security, especially for local journalists.

---

32   International Women's Media Foundation, "Online Violence and Harassment," iwmf.org, accessed February 2, 2023, https://www.iwmf.org/programs/online-harassment/#:~:text=The%20IWMF%20and%20Trollbusters'%20Attacks,profession%20due%20to%20online%20attacks..

We know these risks all too well at Global Press. In a given year, we navigate hurricanes and volcanoes, equipment confiscation by police, traffic accidents, online harassment, and more.

Those risks are standard for local journalists in any location. And yet unlike Global Press, most news organizations offer almost no protection against them.

A Loss of Trust Is Corrosive

The average news consumer does not know the inner workings of journalism. They never know the risks a reporter took or the threats they endured to report a story. Readers don't know that journalists earn low pay, receive minimal benefits, and face a multitude of crises every single day. They are, at most, vaguely aware of the strains the industry puts on journalists and what it takes to report the news, especially from around the world.

At the same time, they likely have some sense that stories are sensationalized or that coverage is incomplete, but only dimly. They may be dissatisfied with the news they receive, but they are usually unable to articulate why and how it falls short.

There is a cumulative effect to these issues. Over time, trust has been lost—both by news consumers and journalists. News consumers don't trust news providers to give them complete, accurate stories. Many journalists don't trust their employers to keep them safe.

All of this points to the simple fact that the model for reporting international news, or frankly any news at all, has become immensely harmful. And for that very reason, it has become unsustainable.

It's time to make a change.

CHAPTER 4

Listen to the Audience

According to a recent study from the Medill School of Journalism at Northwestern University, one-third of US newspapers that existed in 2005 will be out of business by 2025. The percentage may seem high, but it's on trend. Since 2005, more than twenty-five hundred daily and weekly newspapers have already closed.[33]

In 2021, the UN referred to the pandemic as a "media extinction event" after the industry saw more than $30 billion in losses.[34] These losses were primarily felt in remote and rural parts of the US and around the world.

In the places that already received the least coverage, there is now even less. The loss of smaller journalism outlets has created ever-expanding news deserts in which local news is essentially nonexistent.

---

33 Erin Karter, "As Newspapers Close, Struggling Communities Are Hit Hardest by the Decline in Local Journalism," Northwestern Now, June 2022, accessed February 2, 2023, https://news.northwestern.edu/stories/2022/06/newspapers-close-decline-in-local-journalism/.

34 UNESCO, "Journalism, Press Freedom and COVID-19," unseco.org, accessed February 2, 2023, https://en.unesco.org/sites/default/files/unesco_covid_brief_en.pdf

This lack of information equity is only exacerbating the inequities that already exist within these communities.

But even for those news organizations teetering on the brink, there is a hopeful future for journalism. Together, we can turn the tide if we truly understand what our readers want—and are willing to give it to them.

It's Not All Bad News

When I talk to others in the industry, most people agree with me that international journalism could be improved. I have no doubt that most editors and executives would gladly cut down on sensationalism, provide more security for their reporters, and tell deep, comprehensive, accurate stories about everything happening in the world—if they could.

The problem, they always tell me, is that while there may be preferable models to support journalistic quality and employment ethics, these models simply aren't practical today.

But is change truly impractical? Or has journalism simply been unwilling to change? I think it's the latter. That unwillingness to change is wrapped up in old ways of thinking.

When I first met Nicholas Kristof in his office in New York City in 2016, he told me that he doubted audiences would have an appetite for the kind of news Global Press served up day after day. When I spoke to him again in 2022, he said the same thing.

"It is just blindingly clear that people do not read a lot of international development stories," he said. "I did one trip to Yemen. It was incredibly expensive for the *New York Times*, and it was dangerous for me. I did it back to back with a piece about Brett Kavanaugh when he was up for the Supreme Court. And it wasn't just that the Kavanaugh piece had 50 percent more page views or twice as many—it had eight times as many."

That's not an unusual refrain. Carroll Bogert told me that during her time at *Newsweek*, the least-selling covers were always the international covers.

Many news executives have wed themselves to the narrative that this relationship is inevitable: international news can't change and isn't worth the investment because audiences don't care about it enough.

But is that true? Is it that people don't care about the world? Or is it perhaps possible that people are fatigued by the disaster narratives that the media forces upon them? Are they disinterested—or do they just lack better options?

There is a growing body of evidence to suggest the latter. Readers are hungry for stories and information that allow them to see the world differently.

In August 2022, an Associated Press-NORC Center for Public Affairs Research survey revealed that news consumption among people in the United States ages sixteen to forty is high, with 79 percent consuming news daily.[35] While both Gen Z and Millennial news consumers expressed some trust issues with the media, the most important detail of the study lies in what consumers said they wanted from the news: "diverse points of view and to help people understand communities and people unlike their own."

Similarly, according to a Reuters Institute survey conducted in 2022, international news ranked as the second most interesting news topic behind local news. About 40 percent of people under the age of

---

35   APNORC, "Fatigue, Traditionalism, and Engagement: Gen Z and Millennials' Complex Relationship with News," August 2022, accessed February 2, 2023, https://apnorc.org/projects/fatigue-traditionalism-and-engagement-news-habits-and-attitudes-of-the-gen-z-and-millennial-generations/.

35 expressed interest in international coverage, and incredibly, about 60 percent of those over the age of 35 said the same.

People want to better understand the world around them. The lack of interest publishers perceive is due to the static narratives of the world that they peddle. Those narratives don't serve the audience, and the audience knows it. It's time to offer them something different.

Unlock Demand

I'm not trying to oversimplify a complicated business. But what if we just misunderstand what our audiences want—and so continue serving them the wrong thing?

In 2021, Global Press sought to better understand our growing US-based audience. We partnered with Goodwin Simon Strategic Research, an independent public opinion research firm, and Wonder: Strategies for Good, experts in analyzing public opinion research, to help determine what kind of international news stories US-based audiences were most interested in consuming. We presented respondents with a myriad of options for what high-quality international journalism can look like and evaluated the latent demand of these readers for such journalism. The methodology included a large-scale nationwide survey as well as a curated set of in-depth interviews and a multiday asynchronous focus group.

The results were remarkable. Our study established that there is a deep reservoir of untapped demand from readers in the United States, across a wide range of demographics, for international journalism that is local, precise, and representative. It also solved the puzzle of why US-based audiences do not proactively seek out such journalism today.[36]

---

36   Lexmi Parthasarathy and Cristi Hegranes, "Unlocking U.S. Audience Demand for International News," Media Impact Funders, February 2023, accessed February 31, 2023, https://bit.ly/globalpressaudience.

The study demonstrated that readers in the United States are not typically aware that there are alternative models for international reporting aside from the ones that yield static and predictable narratives primarily rooted in crisis. After just a small dose of exposure to media literacy materials, though, audience preferences shift dramatically.

Our report, which I coauthored with Global Press COO Laxmi Parthasarathy, lays out three key findings that emerged from our data, and they offer a way forward for all international news—and the press in general.[37] First, US audiences prefer reading stories about international communities written by local journalists from those communities, rather than by parachute journalists. Second, they value international reporting that is dignified, precise, and avoids tropes and stereotypes. And third, they are hungry for comprehensive coverage that includes historical context and reporting on solutions as well as more serious topics, like human rights and climate change.

These findings present a new way forward for the media industry—and just in time. The end of the pandemic represents an unprecedented opportunity for a readjustment of priorities. This is the perfect time to embark on a new model of international journalism.

"The time is right for it," Carroll Bogert told me. "From #MeToo to George Floyd, we just have a more critical eye on a lot of institutions. And the old institutions of journalistic power are mostly dead. So, if we're rebuilding the media sector, how are we rebuilding it? What about it needs to change? Those are really important questions."

She's right. The world has changed in significant and enduring ways over the last few years. People have become more deeply engaged in many social issues and more willing to investigate systems and structures of power that have long relegated diverse voices and perspectives.

---

37   Ibid.

Journalism's role in this new world is clear: we have to find new ways to tell fuller stories. And the best way to change the story is to change the storyteller. Our aim should be to make all news as proximate as possible—while expanding what we consider "newsworthy."

The old model is broken. Let's listen to our audiences and build back differently.

PART II

A New Vision for International Journalism

CHAPTER 5

Let Local
Reporters Report

Most people in the United States know almost nothing about Zimbabwe. Among those who pay attention to international news, there may be a general understanding that the economy has been on a roller coaster for the last three decades. Some newsreaders may be able to name the former president, Robert Mugabe, who ruled from 1980 to 2017.

But barring a particularly dramatic event—a coup, hyperinflation, or a natural disaster—nothing that happens in Zimbabwe receives coverage because the assumption is that nothing impactful for a "Western" audience happens there. It's hardly surprising, then, that Global Press is one of the only international news organizations with multiple bureaus in the country.

In October of 2018 that limited coverage was particularly unfortunate.

It all started when our news director got a call the morning of October 2 from Gamuchirai Masiyiwa, who goes by Gamu—a senior reporter in our Zimbabwe bureau. She told us that overnight each reporter's bank account had been emptied of US dollars by the government. And it wasn't just our reporters. US dollars had vanished from every citizen's bank account.

Zimbabwe hadn't used its own currency since 2009. (Zimbabwean bond notes were introduced into circulation in 2016, but they were of much less value than a dollar.) In 2018, Zimbabweans were using US dollars for most of their transactions. At the time it was widely believed that banks were a safe place for holding US dollars, even though a serious cash shortage kept citizens from withdrawing any more than small amounts at a time.

Then, overnight on October 1, the government directed banks to, without notice, eliminate US dollars from citizens' bank accounts and replace them with RTGS—a monetary unit that is not tied to a specific currency.

Under normal circumstances, RTGS, a globally used term which stands for "real-time gross settlement," refers to an electronic payment system that occurs between banks. In other words, RTGS isn't a physical currency. You can't withdraw it from an ATM.

That was just the beginning of the confusion. In early October, Clive Mphambela, an executive at the Bankers Association of Zimbabwe, told Gamu that the money now in bank accounts in Zimbabwe should be considered a "local dollar," not a US dollar. Those local dollars were the bond notes. The value of bond notes was fluctuating wildly, and no one really understood what RTGS was. The result? No one knew how much money they had.

"It was chaotic for everyone," Gamu said. "The first thing I thought was, 'How much do I stand to lose?'"

The change spurred immediate and serious consequences. Across the country, shopkeepers refused to accept bond notes as payment.

Since that was the only tangible currency people could now access, the black market for US dollars boomed. Prices skyrocketed. In her reporting, Linda Mujuru, a Global Press senior reporter, found that a bottle of children's medicine that cost $5 in September went for $50 by mid-October.

"We're now panicking, because our money has been reduced to nothing," Clifford Hlatshwayo, 33, told Linda that October of the US dollars he once had in his account.[38]

While our reporters and editors were scrambling to cover the story, I was trying to figure out how to pay our reporters. Global Press isn't a breaking news organization; we focus on feature journalism and long-term coverage. But this was clearly the moment for an exception.

We began reaching out to international news partners, offering them access to our reporters, our reporting, our photos. This was the biggest story in the country, maybe even the continent. Yet, no one seemed eager to pick up the phone to talk details.

As Global Press reporters talked to citizens, local economists, and banking experts on the ground, Krista Karch, Global Press's DC-based news director at the time, reached out to an international expert to get his take on the bizarre overnight cash swap.

She called Steve Hanke, a professor of applied economics at Johns Hopkins University and one of the world's leading experts on hyperinflation.

Hanke called Zimbabwe's actions a "sleight of hand" and was unintimidated to call it theft.

---

38   Linda Mujuru, "Is There a 'Local' Dollar in Zimbabwe? Banks Say Yes," Global Press Journal, October 2018, accessed February 2, 2023, https://globalpressjournal.com/africa/zimbabwe/dollars-gone-overnight-zimbabweans-stagger-new-economic-era/.

"This theft was all under the usual cover of Zimbabwean 'law', a 'law' which isn't worth the paper it's printed on," Hanke wrote to me in an email in 2022, reflecting on the events of 2018.

On the day of the swap Zimbabwe said that the "local currency," the bond notes, were valued at 1:1 with the US dollar. Within a week it was 5:1, Hanke said. And at the close of 2022? "Those fabulous Zimbabwe dollars trade at around 900:1. Since October of 2018, Zimbabwe's dollar has been totally wiped out, losing a stunning 99.9 percent of its value against the US dollar," he said.

As Hanke and others in the global finance world continued to watch the situation unfold, we still had no bites from the international news agencies we'd pitched.

Finally, two weeks into the crisis, we had some interest in the story from National Public Radio. *All Things Considered* host Ari Shapiro had done some previous reporting on Zimbabwe, and on October 17, one of his producers, responded to our pitch. However, by October 19, they'd changed their mind.

"We are going to pass on the interview," the producer wrote to me in an email on that date. "Show editors felt it was just too difficult to explain in a short radio conversation. Thank you very much for the pitch."

Tired of waiting for a partner, we published the story ourselves.

This chaotic story was never fully reported by the international press. BBC, for example, ran a story on it in February of 2019—nearly five months later—in response to a law change that converted debt from US dollars to RTGS.

People Care about Local News Everywhere

That law change was significant.

"In February of 2019, the 'law' was changed when most debts were converted from US dollars to RTGS dollars (ZWL)," Hanke confirmed. "That change was very welcomed by the politicians and generals whose debts were denominated in US dollars."

Gamu's on-the-ground reporting supported the claim.

"It was panic mode for many, but for others, it was actually a prize," Gamu recalled. "For instance, if someone had a mortgage when the system was US dollars, now they had to pay that back in the equivalent of RTGS local currency, which everyone knew was way below the value of the dollar."

The consequences of that 2018 cash swap still linger, Gamu says. "It was the final nail in the box for people's trust in financial institutions," she told me in a 2022 interview.

According to the Economic Freedom of the World 2022 report, Zimbabwe's overall rank is 163 out of the 165 countries covered.[39]

If you aren't a Zimbabwean who saw your hard-earned money disappear overnight in 2018, this may seem like a story you would skim past. After all, though Zimbabwe's GDP is comfortably in the top half of African nations, its size compared to large economies around the globe is small—merely numbering in the tens of billions. How significant were these events to readers in the United States or Europe?

Potentially very significant. A story about a disruption in the Zimbabwean economy can have compounding and cascading effects across Southern Africa. Zimbabwe's an important trading partner

---

39   James Gwartney, Robert Lawson, Joshua Hall, and Ryan Murphy, "Economic Freedom of the World, 2022 Annual Report," Fraser Institute, accessed February 3, 2023, https://www.fraserinstitute.org/sites/default/files/economic-freedom-of-the-world-2022.pdf.

with the far larger South African economy. It also does trade with Singapore, China, and India.

Even more significant, though, is what this story proves about international news in general. Imagine this story taking place in a different country, one where we have been conditioned to understand that people there deserve wealth and stability. If this had happened in France or Canada, would a major US news organization have found it too complicated to explain?

"The mainstream international media's claim that it's too complicated to cover tells you more about the mainstream media than the Zimbabwe theft," Hanke said of the coverage in that 2022 email. "The mainstream media often puts its incompetence on display. That's why I have been able to validate my 95 percent rule: 95 percent of what you read in the press is either wrong or irrelevant."

Were international agencies wrong not to pick up the story? Absolutely. But perhaps the greater revelation here is that these are precisely the kinds of stories news consumers are telling us they want.

They want accurate. They want comprehensive. And they can handle complicated. Rather than shy away from a story like this, we need to tell these stories—not just because international coverage of an issue like this would hold power to account in Zimbabwe, but because taking readers on a journey that allows them to better understand communities outside of their own is precisely what they are telling us they want.

The 2022 Associated Press-NORC research proves that, as does the Global Press survey.[40]

---

40 APNORC, "Fatigue, Traditionalism, and Engagement: Gen Z and Millennials' Complex Relationship with News," August 2022, accessed February 2, 2023, https://apnorc.org/projects/fatigue-traditionalism-and-engagement-news-habits-and-attitudes-of-the-gen-z-and-millennial-generations/.

Still, this audience research is new and requires further development. At the moment, there is a dearth of polling to quantify US readers' preferences for consuming world news. Studies in this area tend to focus on political polarization in the media. For example, a Pew survey in September 2020 revealed that US audience opinions on how the United States should engage with countries around the world are heavily colored by the partisan news sources read by either Democrats or Republicans ensconced in news bubbles.[41] But purposefully built surveys to test readers' appetite for high-quality, international journalism are lacking.

There's a reason for this: doing such research is hard. One difficulty we immediately ran into when trying to evaluate US audience preferences for high-quality international journalism was that US readers did not know what constituted "high quality." All this time news executives, following the well-trodden path of how international stories make the news, have assumed they know what readers want to hear about the world.

The headline result from our findings was that there are, in fact, substantial segments of the US audience that demand high-quality international journalism—once they understand what that means and what is possible.

In our focus group, participants were shown multiple media literacy videos. For example, one video described parachute journalism; another explained the value of proximate coverage. A third video introduced respondents to local journalists reporting for Global Press in news bureaus around the world to give readers a sense of what a "local journalist" looked and sounded like. A dial test recorded

---

41   Mark Jurkowitz, Amy Mitchell, Eliza Shearer, and Mason Walker, "U.S. Media Polarization and the 2020 Election: A Nation Divided," Pew Research Center, January 2020, accessed February 3, 2023, https://www.pewresearch.org/journalism/2020/01/24/u-s-media-polarization-and-the-2020-election-a-nation-divided/.

the instantaneous sentiment of participants. There was a significant shift for participants' preference for local reporters versus parachute journalists.

In the nationwide survey, for example, 67 percent of respondents indicated they believed that a local reporter would understand the context for a story in Democratic Republic of Congo (DRC), compared with just 54 percent of respondents who assessed this would be the case for a foreign reporter—regardless of affiliation with a well-established brand. These results were consistent across each study segment.[42] Once audiences were aware of the option to receive high-quality news from local reporters, they preferred those local journalists regardless of the news outlet shown in the masthead.

Our survey found that it wasn't just the storyteller's identity they cared about either; it was their ability to tell stories that were nuanced, dignified, and precise. Mainstream international news coverage is replete with shorthand phrases, such as "ethnic tensions" and "developing world" that can often mislead readers, perpetuate stereotypes, or force audiences to make assumptions. Our research also found that US-based readers of international news preferred more precise language as well as fuller descriptions of events that represented communities with dignity rather than stereotypes or shorthand. And they preferred it by a large margin.

Two-thirds of respondents found it clearer, more interesting, and more meaningful to read a description explaining the conflict arising from one tribe's livestock destroying another tribe's crops in the DRC's Ituri province. By contrast, the shorthand phrase "ethnic tensions" that was used in mainstream coverage of the issue, which

---

42   Lexmi Parthasarathy and Cristi Hegranes, "Unlocking U.S. Audience Demand for International News," Media Impact Funders, February 2023, accessed February 31, 2023, https://bit.ly/globalpressaudience.

carries little to no substantive meaning without context, did not appeal to most respondents.

And all it took to reach these conclusions was a small dose of additional context and education. The strength of these results suggests that among existing US readers of international news, there is a sizable untapped market for high-quality international journalism that would want stories like the one we covered in Zimbabwe in 2018.

Within Reach

To be sure, the path to improving the quality of international journalism for US audiences remains arduous, but it is not impassable. And the best way to move forward is to allow local journalists to take the lead. They are the ones who can give consumers the nuance and the context they are telling us they want.

The truth is that we've never had a system for international reporting that offered coverage that was locally sourced and comprehensive across topics. Mainstream media has never allowed local journalists in global locations to report the stories of their communities on a large scale.

Our era of interconnectivity is crying out for a news model that provides stories of all types from all places. In our globalized world, people care far more about stories thousands of miles away than they used to—because they feel they have to.

In evaluating coverage from DRC by a white male reporter from the US compared to a local Congolese woman reporter, focus group participants made some key observations that might surprise many traditional publishers.

"There is a disconnect between his name, how he looks, his affiliation, and the focus of the story," said one white woman, 50–77 who identified as liberal.[43] "That's not to say he couldn't report empathetically, but he may not know the right questions to ask. And maybe local people will not feel an affinity with him, so won't be forthcoming." Other participants noted that the local reporter "looked like the people in the photographs" and "would be able to tell me a story he probably could not get."

People, it turns out, care deeply about the nuances of stories from far away places. And unlike the common belief among traditional publishers, many readers take the unprompted step to connect themselves to a story without requiring the journalist to do it for them. For example, the headline of a 2021 story from Lerma, Mexico by Global Press reporter Aline Suárez del Real asked the question "Can Eggshells Save One of Mexico's Most Polluted Rivers?" Focus group participants flocked to the story—as did social media audiences.

People who are concerned about climate change are hungry for articles about solutions, regardless of the dateline location. We all have a stake in our climate, and understanding adaptations emerging anywhere is news. Readers understand their interconnected relationship between communities around the world—even those that we once deemed unworthy of regular coverage. Of course, not every reader will read every article about every event across the world, but the expectation should be that every article will find an audience.

"There is a greater awareness that our lives are connected to events far away," Bobby Ghosh, the former Iraq correspondent who now works for Bloomberg, told me. "Readers find it interesting, and they know it's important to understand those events. Every story should have a paragraph that makes it clear why the reader should care about what's going on somewhere else. Even without it, people know they

---

43   Ibid.

need to care about what's going on in Venezuela because the price they're paying for gas [at home] is directly connected to what's going on in Venezuela."

More than ever, people want to understand what is happening as precisely as they can. This isn't a novel motivation. It's why people have always come to the news. The only difference is that the world people feel they need to understand has become more interconnected.

The reasons to pivot to local reporters as our primary reporters across the world are numerous. Some are ethical—as we will discuss in the next chapter. But others are more fundamental. When we give people the tools they need to understand the world, they are better able to live free, full lives, make better choices, and comprehend their own place in the world. And when news outlets offer that opportunity, readers will respond by returning over and over again for more.

That means any solution to the problems plaguing modern journalism must involve more and better coverage across the world—so that stories like a financial crisis in Zimbabwe aren't ignored for days or even months at a time anymore. And the best way to holistically implement that solution is by giving local journalists the bylines.

Use the Most Proximate Reporter

Even after waiting, Global Press still scooped international organizations on the currency swap in Zimbabwe for one very simple reason: we had established bureaus of local reporters there. Because we had access to local economists and local sources—as well as the traditional experts—we could put together a complete picture of events in a way other, larger news producers couldn't. Because Global Press pairs local reporters with regional or global editors, we're able to produce our news in multiple languages to serve both local and international audiences.

The real value of local journalists to a news organization is that they are on the ground. They know the local context. They speak the language. They have access to a vast number of sources. Put bluntly, they can tell the story better than anyone else. Proximity doesn't just deliver speed on stories; it ensures better reporting and greater accuracy.

And with the slightest explanation, readers feel this way too. In our US audience research, just 12 percent of participants initially said they'd rather hear from local journalists covering their own communities compared to an American parachute journalist.[44] After learning about the pros and cons of both types of reporters, though, participants' attitudes shifted dramatically. By the end, 35 percent of people said they would prefer to hear from local reporters only and 77 percent of people said that they wanted to hear from local reporters in some or all of their international news. Just 13 percent said they still prioritized US journalists' coverage of foreign events.

What was most striking about these results was the way that they encompassed people across age, race, and political affiliation.

"Local perspective is more important to me because it means it would come from the perspective of someone living in the community. They have first-hand experience and knowledge about the issues affecting their community," a Hispanic woman, 35–54, who identified as liberal said in the focus group.

A white man, 35–54, who identified as a conservative concurred. "I agree with my fellow participants. Everyone agrees that local reporters generally are better equipped to cover stories in their own regions/countries. I think that a local reporter does have more

---

44   Ibid.

knowledge and contacts and therefore can provide more detailed and factual stories."

The opportunity to hear from local reporters in times of crisis and day-to-day, rather than only seeing things through the looking glass of parachute journalists, goes beyond even the potential suggested by these focus group responses. It could prove to be truly transformative.

The list of harms that have come from reliance on parachute journalism and a broken bureau system is long and well documented. It took months for the international community to pay attention to the Rwandan genocide, for example. This was at least partly because those who knew what was happening did not have a platform to make those events more widely known.

Local Rwandan journalists knew about the massacres of the Tutsi minority long before it was picked up in the legacy press, just as Zimbabwean journalists knew about the currency swap long before anyone outside the borders was aware anything was going on. In both cases, detailed understanding of the most proximate journalists was second to none for the very reason they were closest to the story.

If we were accustomed to listening when they spoke and giving the stories they wrote a byline, our world would be quite different.

The best way to tell stories is to be there. The term "shoe-leather journalism" might be outdated, but it's time for its return. Across the United States. we're seeing renewed investment in local journalism, and a long list of examples where local journalists get it right when the national press gets it wrong.

After the US Supreme Court overturned *Roe v. Wade* in 2022, a story was circulated about a ten-year-old girl who was raped in Ohio and had to go to neighboring Indiana to receive an abortion. There was an immediate cry of "fake news" from abortion opponents.

It was local journalists in Indiana who investigated, went down to the local courthouse, and proved it was true. And in that single act, a little trust was regained.[45]

We can scale this process across the world. Our audience—our customers—have shown they have interest in this. They will click on articles about stories from around the world. They'll tune in to hear about the events of Zimbabwe and Sri Lanka—if we allow local journalists to report them in authentic, accurate ways.

Greater Context, Greater Understanding

Local reporters can transform not only how much information we get but the type of information we get. At Global Press Institute, the training arm of Global Press that feeds local reporters into our bureaus around the world, we teach our reporters that there are three ways to report every story: in historical context, in breaking context, and in consequence-driven context.

Most news today is reported the second way, in breaking context, that focuses on what is happening right now. Breaking news is a service. But a breaking story that lacks historical context can fracture accuracy. For example, breaking news reports from DRC almost always involves violence or disaster. Stories are written with limited context and result in a similar refrain. DRC is depicted as the lawless, hopeless "rape capital of the world," a moniker the country hasn't been able to shake for more than a decade. What's worse, readers rarely have the opportunity to gain a fuller understanding of why. Breaking news reporting lacks nuance about life in DRC or any sense of the historical context, such as how Belgian colonial rule destabilized the

---

45   Elahe Izadi, "How Local Journalists Proved a 10-Year-Old's Abortion Wasn't a Hoax," Washington Post, July 2022, accessed February 3, 2023, https://www.washington-post.com/media/2022/07/28/ohio-abortion-journalism/.

country with everything from genocide to normalizing forced labor for mining. The opportunity to hear from real people on the ground and see photographs taken by local journalists puts things in sharper context. Understanding this historical nuance and context is often only possible through local journalists.

In the TED Talk by Chimamanda Ngozi Adichie about the dangers of a single story that I referenced in chapter 2, Adichie says:

"The Palestinian poet Mourid Barghouti writes that if you want to dispossess a people, the simplest way to do it is to tell their story, and to start with 'Secondly.' Start the story with the arrows of the Native Americans, and not with the arrival of the British, and you have an entirely different story. Start the story with the failure of the African state, and not with the colonial creation of the African state, and you have an entirely different story."[46]

Too much of our international news starts with "Secondly." And any historian will tell you that such a limited perspective will always fail to deliver the whole story.

The third way to report a story—which to my mind is the most valuable—is nearly impossible without local journalists. Consequence-driven reporting incorporates the first two types of reporting but focuses on the continuing consequences of recent events. This is the kind of reporting we do at Global Press. Our stories always seek to answer the question "So what?"

On May 22, 2021, for instance, Mount Nyiragongo, one of the most dangerous volcanoes in Africa, erupted.

The volcano is located on the outskirts of Goma, the capital of DRC's North Kivu province. The eruption "surprised Florida Baralizi and hundreds of thousands of other residents who lived at the foot of

---

46 Himamanda Ngozi Adichie, "The Danger of a Single Story," TED, 2009, YouTube video, https://www.youtube.com/watch?v=D9Ihs241zeg.

the volcano. Everything she owned—her house, her shop, her clothes, her money, her personal documents, and the field where she grew beans—was reduced to ashes," wrote Noella Nyirabihogo, a Global Press senior reporter in Democratic Republic of Congo.[47]

So far, this could be a disaster story by any parachute journalist, but Noella, an award-winning journalist and accomplished photographer, didn't publish that kind of story. She was on the scene the day of the eruption, taking stunning photographs that circled the world. But she only wrote about the story months later, when the "So what?" became clear.

Noella's story wasn't about the masses of displaced people or the destruction of local homes. Noella's was about why the volcano warning system didn't go off.

"The centerpiece of the country's risk-mitigation program is the Goma Volcano Observatory, which the government established in 1986. After Mount Nyiragongo erupted in 2002, the observatory began monitoring two active volcanoes—Mount Nyiragongo and Mount Nyamuragira—for signs of eruptions. This early warning system was supposed to alert residents to an impending volcanic eruption two weeks before it occurred, allowing them time to evacuate. But when Mount Nyiragongo erupted again in May, there was no warning at all," Noella wrote in her 2021 article, which was published in both French and English.

Noella wanted to know why. And she soon found the culprit—corruption. Scientists working at the observatory claimed that more than $7 million from the European Union, World Bank, and other groups hadn't gone to the project as intended.

---

47   Noella Nyirabihogo, "Officials Trade Blame for Failed Volcano Warning System," Global Press Journal, August 2021, accessed February 3, 2023, https://globalpressjournal.com/africa/democratic-republic-of-congo/officials-trade-blame-failed-volcano-warning-system/.

Célestin Kasereka Mahinda, the observatory's scientific director, told Noella that because of this lack of funding, Mount Nyiragongo hadn't been monitored for seven months prior to the eruption.

"During this whole time, we had no internet connection and were not receiving any real-time data," Mahinda told her.

When I asked Noella why she opted to tell that story, she said simply, "It was the one that most needed to be heard."

Images of lava pouring into the streets circulated cable news and social media for a few days after the eruption. But the story quickly faded into just another African disaster. Noella's story offers a better path—one that incorporates far more context to explain to readers, "So what?" The volcano wasn't just another disaster; it was an example of the type of corruption that the reader understands, the type of corruption stifling important projects around the world. It's the type of corruption that accountability journalism can prevent.

Without that context, we doom our audiences to a reductive worldview that never explains why something happened or how we can prevent it from happening again. And without that context—that "So what?"—our readers have little motivation to tune it for just another disaster story.

CHAPTER 6

A Better Class of Reporting

For as many naysayers as I've encountered over the last seventeen years, including all those who doubt the abilities of local journalists or underestimate the appetite of news consumers, there are many more who have come to celebrate our model.

Since 2006, our journalists have won nineteen journalistic excellence awards. Despite being a relatively small nonprofit organization, our work has been recognized by our peers and appeared in the most prestigious publications.

The reason is simple. Our local journalists, and the incredible team of editors, fact checkers and translators who support them, deliver extraordinarily valuable news about their communities. Because of who our reporters are, our stories are different. Our multilingual model allows us to serve up high-quality stories for local communities and international readers. And most importantly, our stories improve two of the most significant shortcomings of most modern international coverage—accuracy and representative sourcing.

And because of these improvements, both audiences and our publishing partners reap the benefits.

Accuracy

When journalists think about accuracy, they often think about getting the details right. They focus on spelling names correctly, precision in quotes, and double checking the distance between key locations in a story. But accuracy actually starts with the premise of the story we're telling. If the premise of the story is not accurate, the whole story is inaccurate, even if the details are technically correct. And unfortunately, parachute journalists often begin their work from a flawed premise.

Former *New York Times* journalist Don McNeil offers us a particularly egregious example. In 2019, he published a story titled "Diagnoses by Horn, Payment in Goats: An African Healer at Work" about an omushaho wekishaka, or a traditional healer in Uganda.[48] The thesis of his story is laid out in the first sentence: "Samuel Muriisa thinks he is ready for Ebola, but he is not." If the title and the opening line weren't enough to clue you into the fact that the story was written by an outsider to the community, the ominously lit photo at the top of the story shows an older man wearing the pelt of an animal and staring off in the distance, as if waiting for disaster.

The story was published almost exactly two years before McNeil resigned from the *Times* amid controversy about using the n-word,

---

48 Donald G. McNeil Jr., "Diagnoses by Horn, Payment in Goats: An African Healer at Work," New York Times, March 2019, accessed February 3, 2023, https://www.nytimes.com/2019/03/04/health/traditional-healer-africa-ebola.html

among other inappropriate things, while leading a group of high school students on a trip in Peru.[49]

The story sought to draw a connection between West Africa's 2014 Ebola outbreak and cases of Ebola popping up in Uganda's neighboring DRC. In 2014, some suggested that local medicine men had been responsible for hastening the spread of Ebola because they didn't understand it. In 2019, in Uganda, McNeil forced the same premise into an entirely different set of circumstances.

McNeil wrote that Muriisa is "is aware—but only vaguely—that Ebola is raging in the Democratic Republic of Congo, whose border is just 20 miles away." In the article, McNeil suggests that Muriisa doesn't understand the disease that he will soon be responsible for treating. "Traditional healers ... like it or not, are the front lines of rural African medicine," he writes.

McNeil accurately pointed out that across the African continent there are not enough trained medical doctors and hospitals. But then he framed his story around the old tropes of the witch doctor in the bush.

"His office is a thatched mud hut," McNeil wrote, "decorated with shields and antelope horns ... To meet patients, he tops his normal attire—a corduroy jacket and shorts—with a cloak of what appears to be serval cat fur and a headpiece of black and white monkey hair."

The insistence on relying upon stereotypes is unmistakable. The piece reads as an opinion or a travelog, but it was labeled as news. And it drips with disrespect and walks a very flimsy accuracy line.

Intent to learn more about Muriisa, Global Press sent one of our Ugandan reporters, Edna Namara, to Lake Bunyonyi to find him.

---

49   Marc Tracy, "New York Times Reporter Used Racial Slur With Student Group," New York Times, January 2021, accessed February 3, 2023, https://www.nytimes.com/2021/01/28/business/media/donald-mcneil-new-york-times.html.

"I come from Rukiga and [Muriisa] comes from Rubanda. They are different districts now, but before 2018 they were one district," Edna told me when recounting her experience. "I knew he was in the Bunyonyi islands. I'd never been there, but I knew I'd get him."

When I asked her how she was so sure she would find him, she laughed.

"First of all, he's renowned. In traditional Uganda, people like him who are traditional herbalists are quite well known," she said.

She set off from Kampala. When she reached the area, she started asking questions, leveraging her local language and insider access.

"I started in a restaurant where I had my breakfast," she recalled. "I asked them about this gentleman [Muriisa]. I had his photograph from the *New York Times*. They told me to ask people down by the lake. So I went and spoke to some local fishermen. The third person I asked knew him. So I just said, 'May I use your boat?' And off we went."

The brief description of her journey to find Muriisa is filled with so many gems of why local reporters are best equipped to cover their own communities. Her access was extraordinary. But my favorite was the care that she took in ensuring she addressed him in the most respectful way.

"When I got off the boat, I climbed a hill for a few meters. Then I found a girl with a little child. It so happened that she was the granddaughter of the man I was looking for," she said. "Those traditionalists have a special way they are referred to with respect, so I first had to be oriented. I asked the girl how to refer to him. I said, 'Do you call him "Mugurusi,"'—meaning 'village elder'—'or do you call him "Doctor?"' She told me to call him Mugurusi. Then she led me to him, and he was so happy to greet me."

When Edna arrived, Muriisa was not draped in furs. He was wearing Dockers and a linen blazer. When Edna asked him about the *Times* story, he was confused. He said he'd been clear with the reporter's translator that no one would come to him to treat Ebola, let alone a person from DRC. That was improbable for a number of reasons. First, he'd rarely seen Congolese people here. Second, Muriisa's practice had a clear focus. People primarily came to him to treat one thing—erectile dysfunction. (This important detail was absent from McNeil's story.)

The premise of McNeil's story began to seem increasingly flawed. He had written that cases of Ebola were popping up in DRC, but misled readers about the proximity. While it's true that the border is twenty miles away, when Global Press research editor Bennett Hanson plotted the cases of Ebola in DRC with Muriisa's location, they were, in fact, more than a hundred miles away. And the trip to get there would include a dangerous journey through Virunga National Park, a border crossing into a country where people speak a multitude of different languages, and at least one boat ride. An alternate route would be a trip through a forest actually called "the Impenetrable Forest."

It's hard to see how McNeil missed all of this. But his lack of familiarity with the region may have been a factor. Afterall, he did not find Muriisa on his own. He was tagging along with some visiting members of a Canadian charity, Bridge to Health, which was offering routine medical and dental care in nearby villages. They were not doing any work related to Ebola, as McNeil's article admits. Muriisa's interview with McNeil was translated by a local dentist.

In other words, he had no connection to the village, no experts on the disease in the area with him, and no ability to directly understand the people he was interviewing. He had an amateur translator and a group doing charity medical work.

After Edna returned from her trip with all of the details, which included some complaints from one of Muriisa's wives—polygamy is common there—that McNeil had misquoted her, we wrote to the *Times*.

Initially encouraged by the prompt response and pledge to look into our request, we were soon back in familiar territory. Six days later, a response from Michael Mason, deputy science editor read, in part: "Thanks very much for your letter and for sharing your concerns. After close review, and following consultation with Mr. McNeil, we cannot agree that the article should be retracted, nor that it is in error."

The result was frustrating but not surprising.

"He parachuted there and created his own fear-based story that made no sense," our research editor Bennett said.

I share this story not to dredge up wrongdoings of another famous, even if now discredited, parachuter, but to point out the inequity of the reporting and how that manifests in our adherence to accuracy. Imagine a *Times* story suggesting that a specific pharmacist in California may do harm at some point in the future because he's ill-equipped to treat a potential outbreak of a disease not yet in his community. That article would, of course, never go to print. And if it did, it would be followed by lawsuits. McNeil's article was accusatory and based on a far-fetched premise never likely to play out. The only difference is that the man at the center of the story was never supposed to have access to the published piece. He was never supposed to be able to hold McNeil accountable.

A story like McNeil's is only possible when the journalist, the editor, the publisher, and the reader don't have the context or the access to get a fuller version of the story. It only gets published when accuracy is deprioritized and those who could correct the record are disenfranchised.

If the *New York Times* had kept Don McNeil at home and connected to a local journalist like Edna in the first place, the editors would have known the story's framing was foolish from the start. She could have told them that it was unlikely and illogical for any Congolese person, let alone one dying of Ebola, to turn up at Muriisa's place. She would have described the self-defined parameters of Muriisa's practice and confirmed that he would never try to treat an Ebola patient. And in that improbable story's place, she could have told them about a dozen stories of things actually happening in Uganda—accurate, valuable stories that could truly benefit readers.

Sourcing

Much of a journalist's ability to tell a story relies on who they can access to get the facts and the details of the events they're covering. And who the journalist is determines who they have access to. For international news, as in all coverage, the best journalist for any story is the one with proximate access to the people and places relevant to the story.

There is an evidence-based correlation between who works in a newsroom and who is quoted and featured in stories. When we send elite outsiders to tell the stories of far away communities, we increase the likelihood that those stories will be inequitably sourced because who they have access to is extremely limited. And that sourcing is just as responsible for reinforcing global stereotypes as the stories themselves.

Consider the news coverage of Haiti. As the country navigates ongoing lawlessness, most people quoted on the subject by major news organizations are human rights experts based in the United States. Rebuilding experts interviewed after an earthquake tend to be from the United States or Canada too. This sourcing is most convenient for the journalist in the United States, who likely doesn't speak

French, almost certainly doesn't speak Creole, and may or may not have spent any time in Haiti.

These sourcing choices, made due to lack of authentic access, have significant consequences. They perpetuate the narrative that Haitians are helpless and can't speak or act on their own behalf. This is, of course, untrue and unfair. But by not featuring Haitian people and Haitian experts in stories, audiences are passively guided into these stereotypical assumptions.

Moreover, this type of sourcing necessarily limits the perspective shared in the reporting. These sources may add value, but they are not Haitian or in Haiti. They lack immediate context.

For South African journalist Lesley Wroughton, local sourcing is the key to equitable storytelling. Wroughton spent twenty-six years at Reuters and is now a contributor to the *Washington Post* from South Africa.

"You have got to find those ordinary voices," she told me. "A lot of local reporters complain that international news organizations just go to the NGOs and the international organizations for quotes. Those organizations are good for statistics and context, but there's no way you can base a whole story just on talking to people from the UN. No way."

And when they can't get those ordinary voices, it means they're not getting the whole story.

In the course I teach at Georgetown, I designed a faux parachute assignment within DC for my students. They're asked to do a story on a sensitive topic in an immigrant community where they have no connection and do not speak the language.

The assignment is deeply uncomfortable. In the fall 2022 semester, I sent students into three communities just days after the fourth COVID-19 booster was approved to ask if specific subsets of immigrant populations, from El Salvadorian women to young Chinese people—planned to take it.

While most students completed the assignment, a few emailed me before it was due saying they had serious reservations that ranged from feeling like they were racially profiling to accuracy concerns over cherry-picking information—all valid concerns. (I had a backup assignment ready for those students.)

Once the assignments were handed in, I asked students to raise their hands if they were proud of the stories they had submitted. No hands went up. Did anyone feel the stories were accurate? No hands. Did they feel the stories portrayed people in these communities with dignity and precision? Once again, no hands.

This little taste of parachute journalism was intended to prove a point. When the journalist lacks total access to a community, the resulting coverage will, almost by definition, be inaccurate and based on the assumptions of outsiders.

There's No Excuse

There are two common objections I hear from those who have reservations about making a move toward local reporters around the world. First, they tell me, changing the model to hire local journalists is too difficult or expensive. And second, local journalists are too biased and too poorly trained.

If not for these issues, they say, perhaps greater reliance on local journalists would be possible.

Lucky for us, then, that these points aren't particularly valid.

Taking the former objection first, basic economics shows that using local journalists can fit any reasonable news budget—especially when supported in lieu of the expensive price tag to send a big-name parachute journalist anywhere. Local journalists can offer extraordinary context and access at an affordable price, even when we pay them well and provide for their security.

The logistics of language, the most common basis for the "it's too hard" complaint, can also be easily overcome. At Global Press, English is not a requirement for any of our reporters. Only about 30 percent of our reporters speak and write in English. That's intentional. The inability to speak English is one of the greatest barriers to entry for journalists around the world.

In order to ensure language equity, we have a well-honed team of translators and interpreters who are part of the Global Press Accuracy Network. Together, they help ensure that our stories are accurate and available to both local and international audiences. We assign multiple translators to each story, ensuring that each is translating into their native language. We assign a separate team of interpreters to facilitate editorial discussion. On average, the cost of putting such a team on one story rarely tops $600.

Even with the costs of editing and translating, dozens of stories from local journalists wouldn't come anywhere near to the cost of sending McNeil to Uganda, for example.

Building an in-house translation network has significant advantages, says Terry Aguayo, Global Press's managing editor.

"We have a rigorous recruitment process that is focused not only on finding the best translators and interpreters but also ensuring their values are well aligned with our own," Terry told me. "Having our own network means that team understands the work we do very well. They are from the regions we cover, have native proficiency in the languages we publish in, and just as importantly, believe in our mission of creating a more informed world. That perspective is essential when producing a news product that is accurate, precise, and inclusive."

The more insidious assumption is the second one—that local journalists have ethical or talent limitations that would prevent them from becoming the storytellers of record. Many assume that a local journalist can't provide accurate stories because they lack the language, writing skills, and education to report a story to the standards we set at major publications in the United States. Others assume that local journalists are by definition biased or corrupt.

This is often expressed elliptically—perhaps because those saying it realize how it must sound. They tell me that journalism is "different" in different places. Or that it wouldn't be fair to expect local journalists to meet "our standards" of accuracy and ethics.

Of course, standards and styles for journalism differ across the world. And just as standards and style differ at Buzzfeed and the *New Yorker*, teaching a journalist to adhere to a publication's style is part of onboarding any new reporter. That argument just doesn't hold weight.

"I've heard the argument in newsrooms," Wroughton told me of the assumption that local reporters aren't as good. "Like all journalists, local journalists need an editor. And sometimes stories need some background added if the reporter isn't used to writing for an international audience."

As someone who has trained hundreds of local journalists over the years, I agree. Teaching someone to write for an international audience is a skill. But it's hardly rocket science.

Ghosh says he experienced this bias firsthand when he was the editor in chief of the *Hindustan Times*, India's second largest newspaper.

"We had a syndication service, but very few publications in the Western world took anything from us," he said. "Some of it had to do with the fact that we were not writing for a Western audience—I think that's the most charitable explanation. The less charitable explanations would include that they'd question our credibility or just held the general assumption that local reporters don't meet their exalted Western standards."

Ghosh's experience is by no means rare. A major broadcaster in the United States once told me that our reporter's voice had "too much texture" to be featured on air. And in our audience research, some readers shared the same general perception that quality or ethics were somehow compromised when hearing from local reporters. "I feel they already have an opinion if it's their own country, and they'd be less objective," one white female focus group participant told us in 2021.

Scratch under the surface, though, and these objections are nothing more than a lazy dismissal of the experiences of people in communities outside of our own.

An easy smell test is a simple question: Does the reverse make sense?

Do people in the United States crave their news written by Guatemalan people because we are too biased to report on our own country well? Would an Egyptian reporter who doesn't speak English and who came to the United States for six days help us better understand the major issues of our day? Of course not.

Far from enabling bias, changing the byline to a local journalist enables a far more compelling, accurate, well-sourced—and ethical— form of journalism.

And this isn't the only ethical issue local journalists alleviate.

CHAPTER 7

Check Your Ethics

Have you heard of Damien Mander?

As far as most international news outlets are concerned, Damien Mander is a hero. An Australian Iraq war veteran and well-known conservationist, he runs a group called Akashinga, an all-female anti-poaching organization in Zimbabwe. These rangers patrol Zimbabwe's Phundundu Wildlife Area in the Zambezi Valley.

Mander initially made headlines when he chose to staff this anti-poaching group with local women from around the wildlife area. According to the group's marketing materials, all the women rangers have experienced some form of violence or abuse in their past. Mander also says, and there is some evidence to support this, that they are successful in their antipoaching efforts too.

It's a compelling story. No wonder, then, that in 2019, *National Geographic* magazine commissioned a piece on Mander and the

Akashinga rangers.[50] A parachute reporter and photographer visited their camp for a few days. A year later, National Geographic Films made a documentary about the group, executive produced by three-time Academy Award winner James Cameron and directed by Maria Wilhelm.

Theirs was a powerful and heartwarming story. But that's not what Global Press reporter Kudzai Mazvarirwofa found when she covered Akashinga months before the National Geographic crew stepped foot in the area, back in 2018.

When Kudzai arrived at the camp, it was clear that things were not OK.

"Two hours in, there was talk about a cleansing ceremony in the village," Kudzai told me. "A cleansing ceremony is only done to ward off bad spirits or avenging spirits. I asked Damien about it, and he brushed it off."

Kudzai was also curious about the arrival of a Harare-based therapist who happened to be visiting the camp at the same time she was.

"The next day I started talking to the rangers, and he was hovering around," she recalled. "He told me which rangers to talk to, guiding me to the ones who spoke English. I told him that wasn't necessary."

Unlike the reporters who would come to stay with the rangers the following year, though, Kudzai speaks Shona. When Mander and the other leaders weren't around, Kudzai could freely ask questions. She had the language, the cultural context, and the trust of the women to push beyond Mander's narrative and get to the truth.

Away from Mander, Akashinga rangers admitted something horrible: three members of their team were dead.

---

50 Lindsay N. Smith, "Why Zimbabwe's Female Rangers Are Better at Stopping Poaching," National Geographic, June 2019, accessed February 3, 2023, https://www.nationalgeographic.com/magazine/article/akashinga-women-rangers-fight-poaching-in-zimbabwe-phundundu-wildlife-area.

Two of their fellow women rangers and one male sergeant were part of a group patrolling a portion of the roughly 230,000 acres that Mander says the unit secures. When they came upon a waterway, some members of the group pushed through the water instead of climbing on the rocks that flanked it. One ranger, who couldn't swim, began to struggle, at which point, her sergeant and another ranger went back to help her. All three drowned.

In the weeks that followed Kudzai's visit to the camp, Global Press tried to get a statement from Mander. He was initially vague and reluctant to talk.

Finally, he responded, saying that the week the rangers died was "the worst week" of his life.[51]

"It's a dangerous job, and to lose people in an accident, as opposed to in an operation—if it's possible to be more tragic, it is more tragic," Mander told Global Press in 2018.

And it was tragic because negligence was involved. At least one of the rangers had not been trained to swim. That's a key skill for ranger training programs, according to guidelines published by the World Wildlife Federation and other organizations.[52] Mander's organization, the International Anti-Poaching Foundation, which runs Akashinga, is listed as a contributor to the guidelines.

Kudzai hit on other signs of questionable preparation too. During training exercises, the women appeared poorly trained:

---

51   Kudzai Mazvarirwofa, "Women Rangers Pursue Poachers in Zimbabwe While Debate Ensues Over Anti-Poaching Tactics," Global Press Journal, October 2018, accessed February 3, 2023, https://globalpressjournal.com/africa/zimbabwe/australian-training-women-stop-poachers-zimbabwe-right-man-job/.

52   World Wildlife Fund, "New Field Ranger Training Guidelines Could Save the Lives of Those on the Front Line of the Poaching Battle," February 2017, accessed February 3, 2023, https://wwf.panda.org/wwf_news/?291871/field5Franger5Ftraining5Fguidelines.

awkward when loading guns and performing seemingly staged hand-to-hand combat exercises.

That wasn't all. Kudzai uncovered inconsistencies in the narrative around Akashinga. Many of the women Kudzai spoke to said they had never experienced domestic violence or other forms of abuse, counter to the marketing claims of the group.

Our story, which was published in English and available for free online in October of 2018, presented a balanced and important picture of Akashinga.[53] It detailed some of their successes, but it also called into question the ethics and the safety of an organization that purported to empower women so they could protect their country's wildlife.

So imagine our surprise when seven months later, one of the world's most credible news magazines followed our story and presented a glowing portrayal of Mander and the organization.[54] There was no mention of the training accident or the dead women.

"The issue with Damien Mander is that he is a hulking charismatic Australian guy—a former sniper who served in Iraq, then turned protector of elephants and employer of African women. And he is vegan," says Bennett, Global Press's research editor who spent a lot of time with Kudzai researching Mander after her trip to the camp in 2018.

Kudzai agrees.

"His story fits the savior narrative," she said. "He's 'helping' African women and African animals. And he's white."

53 Kudzai Mazvarirwofa, "Women Rangers Pursue Poachers in Zimbabwe While Debate Ensues Over Anti-Poaching Tactics," Global Press Journal, October 2018, accessed February 3, 2023, https://globalpressjournal.com/africa/zimbabwe/australian-training-women-stop-poachers-zimbabwe-right-man-job/.

54 Lindsay N. Smith, "Why Zimbabwe's Female Rangers Are Better at Stopping Poaching," National Geographic, June 2019, accessed February 3, 2023, https://www.nationalgeographic.com/magazine/article/akashinga-women-rangers-fight-poaching-in-zimbabwe-phundundu-wildlife-area.

Considering his profile, it was much easier to tell a heroic story over an accurate one. But making that choice comes with some very troubling ethical costs.

Who Gets to Tell Your Story?

Our reporting on Mander and Akashinga is an excellent example of the value local journalists bring to providing more accurate, comprehensive reporting. But it's also an example of how parachute journalists, for all their good intentions, fail to provide the complete stories that people actually need.

The most troubling part of the Mander story for Kudzai is what the unquestioned praise of Akashinga means for the people living in the Zambezi Valley. "Black Africans living in rural areas are a forgotten demographic," Kudzai told me in 2022. "They're portrayed as uneducated and poor. And they don't speak English, so for foreign journalists, they're easy to pass by."

Lindsay Smith, the National Geographic correspondent who wrote the 2019 story about Mander, didn't respond to requests to be interviewed for this book. I wish she had. I wanted to ask her if she had seen Kudzai's story. And if she hadn't, I wanted to know if it would have changed the way she approached her coverage.

Because while it's important to tell positive stories about people doing good things in the world, readers—both local and in the United States—needed to know the sort of information in Kudzai's story far more. They need nuance and accuracy, not hero worship.

News consumers deserve more than tropes and stereotypes in international coverage. And local people who appear in the glossy pictures of these mainstream media stories deserve to recognize themselves in those stories. Yet when narratives and story priorities are

determined from afar, tropes, stereotypes, and undignified representation are often the result. From thousands of miles away, everyone can
look like a hero, a villain, or a victim—but that simplistic framing
doesn't serve anyone. In fact, it often reduces complex individuals
into caricatures.

In my class at Georgetown, I introduce my students to a Global
Press reporter on two different slides. On the first slide, I show a
photo of her with the text on the slide says that she comes from a
war-torn country. It gives some physical characteristics (she's barely
five feet tall); personal details of the sort commonly included when
reporting on women around the world (she had a baby in her teens
and survived domestic abuse); and it frames her work as a reporter
in a classic rags-to-riches framework (prior to becoming a journalist,
she sold tomatoes).

Then I flip to slide two.

Here, students have the opportunity to read the professional
biography she wrote about herself. On this slide, the very same woman
is presented as an award-winning reporter who specializes in covering
human rights. Her long list of professional awards and accolades are all
listed. This slide also ends with a different kind of dramatic detail—
she is the most-syndicated journalist in Global Press history.

Which one is true?

In stark terms, they both are, but we all know that the first slide is
a more common, more familiar way to present an African woman, by
her worst days and least powerful attributes. Journalists and publishers tend to feel more entitled to personal information about people
in other countries, even as we dismiss their individual relevance. We
would never take the liberty to define a *Washington Post* reporter by a
teenage pregnancy and her height. So why would it be acceptable to
describe an African reporter this way? And along those lines, would

National Geographic have ignored the deaths Global Press discovered if the drowned were European tourists?

The troubling assumption is clearly that people in far away locations deserve less consideration all around. Parachute journalists often feel entitled to describe the people in their stories as they wish. They feel entitled to ignore those people unless their sad story serves a narrative purpose. And they certainly feel entitled to force a lens, a foreign lens, on them that fits the overall dominant narrative back home.

When a parachute journalist is assigned to go into a community to tell a certain story, they tend to find that story whether or not it reflects reality. They publish it, whether or not it is accurate.

We saw this in chapter 3, when the Northwestern professors who contacted Indian journalist Neha Dixit to work as a fixer on a specific story they'd already decided on from seventy-five hundred miles away. They just needed Dixit to fix up the details for them.[55]

The same is true of McNeil's treatment of Muriisa—the traditional healer we met in the last chapter—who was a means to a narrative end. Muriisa was never a threat. There was a near 0 percent chance that he would ever have a single Congolese Ebola patient at his door, but that didn't matter to McNeil.

On a broader and more destructive scale, we can see this trend at play in coverage of Muslims and Muslim communities over the last two decades. Stories about Muslims almost always focus on violence and terrorism. Details about individuals almost always connect to poverty or extremism. There aren't people in these stories; there are caricatures.

---

55 Priyanka Borpujari, "The Problem with 'Fixers,'" Columbia Journalism Review, Summer 2019, accessed February 2, 2023, https://www.cjr.org/special_report/fixers.php.

In our interconnected world, these flimsy narratives have consequences. In particular, they create a vortex of selective distortion—the idea that something that has been a story before is more likely to be a story again—as every story has to further support the assumptions that previous stories have already embedded. Movies, TV, and—crucially here—journalism has promulgated a version of the world in which some people save, and some people need to be saved. Some people are intelligent, educated, and powerful, and others are weak, ignorant, and incapable of changing their own lives. Some people deserve our respect. Others can only hope for our pity.

These well-worn stereotypes are part of the reason people dismiss the potential impact of local journalists in this industry. Global narratives have never allowed for the possibility of their power or utility. This is especially true of local women around the world. So when I suggest they are the future of our craft, many find the idea easy to dismiss.

I've been known to make people uncomfortable when they ask me to "describe Global Press's beneficiaries." In a traditional philanthropic setting, people are expecting a dramatic depiction of the women journalists of Global Press. They are expecting to hear a classic tale of poor women in faraway places benefiting from their donations. They are surprised when instead I say: "You are the beneficiary of our work. Thanks to these incredible women journalists, you now have the opportunity to see the world differently."

This is why elevating the platforms of all local journalists is an ethical necessity for the future of our profession. We owe it to our readers and those at the center of events to provide more nuanced reporting. People deserve to be described and understood fully. They deserve to see their community reflected accurately. They deserve access to accurate information over simplistic and stereotypical tales.

And the best way to do that is by allowing those within the community to tell the stories. I've been doing this for nearly twenty years now. Believe me when I say that the end result isn't biased coverage—it's profound coverage. And it's an opportunity to see the world as it truly is.

Information Is a Human Right

People have a right to recognize themselves in stories. I believe that to my core. And I've built my organization around that belief. At Global Press our local audiences have always been our priority audience. That means that we report and publish in the languages that our local readers speak so that they have the opportunity to hold us to account. Then, English-language versions of stories are widely distributed to other news outlets around the world so international audiences can benefit from the dignified and precise coverage of their communities.

But there's another and equally important reason we publish in the local language. These communities have a right to be informed about what is happening around them.

That's not the perspective many international news outlets bring to their coverage. For them, the local people in stories are a means to an end. And are not considered part of the audience.

Most news organizations are commercial entities beholden to advertisers. I get it. The reality that audiences in Mongolia or Zimbabwe can't contribute to a news outlet's bottom line is real. Add language barrier and limited internet access, and it's no wonder that local people never receive access to a foreign correspondent's stories. Again, I get it. But we still have to understand the consequences of that choice.

When parachute stories are written exclusively in English and are only available on the internet, or even behind a paywall, that means that these stories are about people they are never for. To parachute into a media market that is known to lack access to free, fair information and choose not to make your story available locally is extractive. The story is reported—sources are contacted, interviews are completed, research is done, and copy is written—all for the sake of educating those audiences in the United States or Europe. This smacks of colonial methods that have held back too much of the world for centuries.

It doesn't have to be this way. Making local publishing partnerships is free. As I detailed in the last chapter, getting a piece translated by a professional costs a few hundred bucks.

We can immediately recognize the moral imperative of access to information when the stories take place within our own borders. Recently, the *New York Times* translated a story about education within Hasidic schools in New York City into the Yiddish used by that community.[56] The point was to make sure this information was available to those who most needed to know that the schools weren't providing basic skills like reading and mathematics to the students.

The parents with children in those schools had a right to accurate information about the schools so that they could make the best choices for their kids. This is equally true for the women in the Zambezi Valley. They have a right to know if the group recruiting from their community is providing the training they need to survive on patrols.

This is why every piece should be available in the community where it was reported, in the local language of the place.

---

56 Eliza Shapiro and Brian M. Rosenthal, "In Hasidic Enclaves, Failing Private Schools Flush With Public Money," New York Times, September 2022, accessed February 3, 2023, https://www.nytimes.com/2022/09/11/nyregion/hasidic-yeshivas-schools-new-york.html.

Access to accurate information is a human right. In the absence of accurate information, we are less free. We make less informed choices. It's easy to recognize this on a larger scale. We know the dangers of "fake news" and repressive societies that throttle journalism. In fact, the rise of authoritarianism across the world right now is all about restricting access to information to retain control of the masses.

Yet we journalists repress information ourselves by delivering flimsy international narratives intended to only serve our audiences in New York or London. In our globalized world, our readers and viewers absolutely need to know when currency is manipulated in Zimbabwe and how antipoaching organizations treat their rangers. But people in those places have a right to benefit from those stories too.

In 2022, the *Washington Post* published a story about a priest who had raped a young nun in Democratic Republic of Congo.[57] The story's headline revealed the horrific detail that this priest was still being protected by the local bishop and continued to perform Mass.

This is obviously a story of importance to everyone, particularly Catholics, and it makes sense that the *Post* would publish this in English for its US readers. But who needs to know about that priest most? It isn't the Catholics of Los Angeles or Boston. It's the members of that priest's congregation in DRC. Despite this obvious fact, the story wasn't made available in French.

Similarly, if Don McNeil felt there was a real risk to Ugandans that Ebola would spread from DRC, surely the first duty of the *New York Times* was to publish that story in Rukiga, the language spoken by the people in that area.

---

57   Chico Harlan, "A Congo Teen Alleged Rape by a Priest. She Had to Flee. He Can Still Say Mass.," New York Times, July 2022, accessed February 3, 2023, https://www. washingtonpost.com/world/2022/07/15/congo-catholic-priest-sex-abuse/.

By publishing in local news outlets and in local languages, the local residents could be better informed, and they could take proper precautions to protect themselves. And that would be a far more ethical and inclusive form of coverage.

A Virtuous Cycle

Though news consumers might not be able to articulate these ethical missteps, they are central to the trust issue at the heart of journalism today. Together, they add up to the reason people simply choose to tune news out. They have a vague sense that all news, on some level, is "fake."

Of course, that's not the case. But when people don't recognize themselves in stories or when news seems to be extracted from communities for the benefit of others, it's easier to believe.

We've seen this play out in the United States in recent years. In fact, I've seen it play out in my own family. My dad has always been politically conservative. He voted for Donald Trump in 2016. And throughout the Trump presidency, I watched as he became more and more outraged by the news. He didn't see himself represented in cable news or in the major daily papers. He wasn't a wing nut. He didn't have posters of Trump as Rambo hanging on his wall. He doesn't support Proud Boys. And he's never attended a MAGA rally. He knew the news wasn't telling him the full story because he couldn't see a reflection of himself anywhere in the coverage.

This same phenomenon plays out across races, cultures, and even whole continents. The more readers encounter stereotypes and bias, the more they will turn away from that news, unable to square it with their own identities and experiences.

The answer to this seemingly intractable problem is simple and comes in just two parts. First, we must invest in journalists who represent the communities they cover. In the same way that Kudzai was able to get a deeper, truer story by being able to sit down with people and converse in a shared culture and language, we would better understand inner cities and rural communities (let alone people in Mozambique or Laos) if we had reporters who hailed from there. And second, we must tell stories that are as much for the communities we're covering as for our international audiences. That means we must focus on providing information to those who need it most in a way that allows them to recognize themselves in the story.

We live in a world in which access to high-quality information is possible. We live in a time when people care about social justice. As coverage improves, a publication can enter a virtuous cycle in which trust compounds and readership is gained.

CHAPTER 8

Building Representative Newsrooms

Global Press works exclusively with local women journalists around the world. They work in our independent news bureaus and all of them are from the communities that they cover. Of course, men are an important and valued part of our workforce, but the point person investigating and interviewing on the ground is always a woman.

I know this strikes some as odd. From publishers to philanthropists, the most common question I've been asked since 2006 is "Why women?"

The fuller question that I think they mean to ask is this: If the goal is to tell more comprehensive stories from areas of the world that receive limited coverage, why limit the number of people you're training to tell them?

The answer is simple. In journalism, representation matters. And intentionally building a representative workforce requires knowledge of two things: Who lives in this community? And who is already working in journalism there?

When we go to a country where we want to build a bureau, these questions guide us. First, we look at the composition of the community. We breakdown the urban and rural populations, the differences in educational background and socioeconomic statuses, the tribal power dynamics, and the place religion, race, or caste has in the community. In short, we want a clear picture of this society—who lives there. Then, we do an assessment of the media in that place. Who controls the media? Who works in the media? Who gets quoted by the media?

With answers to all of those questions, we can finally work to answer the most important question of all: Who's missing? Who lives in the community but is absent from newsrooms and news stories?

Across the world, the reality is always the same: the media of any place are controlled by the elite. That elite looks different in every community, but whoever represents the elite in that specific context controls the media, owns the media, and works in the media.

This necessarily limits coverage. The majority of the elite are almost always members of the dominant groups in that culture. And that means they work for people like them, speak to people like them, and cover stories that people like them tend to read.

As we assess the discrepancy between who lives in a community and who works in that community's media, there is a plain first observation—women are underrepresented in almost every media market on earth. Where they do find jobs in journalism, too many are still relegated to the lifestyle pages.

As we saw in chapter 6, there is a correlation between who works in a newsroom and who is quoted in stories. According to the Women's Media Center, two-thirds of international news is reported by men.

It's hardly surprising, then, that women make up just 24 percent of sources in the news.

In other words, Global Press hires women to report the news because they rarely have a powerful presence in local newsrooms in the communities where we work. By training and hiring women in these places, we're helping to diversify the entire market. Because our stories are available for free republication by local news outlets, larger audiences can benefit from our diverse newsroom and the diverse sourcing and stories that we produce.

We're known for hiring women, but the truth is that's just the beginning of our approach to building representative newsrooms. We hire people with disabilities, people from the LGBTQ+ community, as well as people of different geographies and educational and socio-economic backgrounds within the country. It all matters. It all helps ensure our coverage is representative of the community.

Of course, it's not a perfect science. Each country requires its own representation assessment. And sometimes populations histori-cally absent from the local journalism scene pass on the opportunity to join up.

We acknowledge the missing perspectives in our newsrooms and consistently work to assess and recruit new journalists. Still, our stories continue to be well read and widely syndicated because they are so different from the stories that fill other news organizations' pages. Our ability to tell those missing stories is thanks to the unique group of people who intentionally fill our newsrooms.

Why Diversity Efforts Fail

Diversifying newsrooms is not a new goal. Yet, in the United States, as in much of the rest of the world, diversity efforts have been largely unsuccessful, despite decades of emphasis.

In 2001, Tom Rosenstiel and Bill Kovach published *The Elements of Journalism*, a journalism school classic, which outlines the core principles of the modern craft.[58] The book emerged as a result of their discussions with twenty-five journalists over the previous years, covering the industry between the Watergate and Whitewater scandals.

There was a growing sense that trust was waning and that dollars and technology were impending challenges. To combat these difficulties, Rosenstiel and Kovach laid out in plain terms the principles and the responsibilities of modern journalism.

Among their principles, they mention the importance of the identity of the journalist. Breaking significantly from the myth that journalists are robotic beings capable of total objectivity, they argued that a journalist's identity informs and even improves their practice.

Rosenstiel elaborated on the topic for Kathleen McElroy, director of the School of Journalism and Media at the University of Texas at Austin, in a piece she wrote for the Poynter Institute for Media Studies in 2019.[59]

"There is no implication that if you are an African American journalist or Hispanic or Jewish or Buddhist that you deny that or blot it out. Just the opposite. It informs your journalism. It becomes descriptive, as we say, not limiting," he wrote to McElroy in an email.

---

58 Bill Kovach and Tom Rosenstiel, *The Elements of Journalism*, (New York City: Crown, 2021).

59 Kathleen McElroy, "Why Don't Newsroom Diversity Initiatives Work? Blame Journalism Culture," Poynter., August 2019, accessed February 3, 2023, https://www.poynter.org/ethics-trust/2019/why-dont-newsroom-diversity-initiatives-work-blame-journalism-culture/.

"An African American journalist doesn't cover only African American matters. Nor does she deny her ethnicity. It should make her a better journalist. Just as her gender does. But she wouldn't put it ahead of her job. Her knowledge helps her do it better."

In recent years some legacy media outlets have loosened their grip on their worship of the term objective and have begun to acknowledge that a reporter's identity is an asset, not something to be checked at the door.

"At *the Times*, for example, our attitudes have changed," Kristof told me. "Where we used to think that it was a conflict of interest for somebody to be from a country, like British reporter Alan Cowell was for a time not allowed to cover Britain. And that attitude has clearly changed now."

Kristof cited media coverage of China as one of the best examples of this shift. In this case, it's been one of necessity. Mainstream media outlets are often dependent on Chinese and Chinese American journalists who speak the languages and have deep context and insight into the country; otherwise, it would be nearly impossible to cover well.

Despite general consensus on this topic, though, efforts to increase diverse voices in journalism have been historically ineffective. In a 2022 Pew Research Center poll of twelve thousand journalists in the United States, 52 percent said their newsroom lacks racial diversity.[60] For example, at Gannett, a media company whose portfolio includes USA Today and dozens of local media outlets across the United States and the United Kingdom, their 2022 inclusion report, shows negligible progress toward diversifying its workforce. In 2020,

---

60   Carrie Blazina, Amy Mitchell, Mark Jurkowitz, and Jacob Liedke, "Journalists Give Industry Mixed Reviews on Newsroom Diversity, Lowest Marks in Racial and Ethnic Diversity," Pew Research Center, June 2022, accessed February 3, 2023, https://www.pewresearch.org/journalism/2022/06/14/journalists-give-industry-mixed-reviews-on-newsroom-diversity-lowest-marks-in-racial-and-ethnic-diversity/.

74 percent of its total workforce was white. By 2022, that number had crept down to 72 percent.

With major diversity initiatives failing to see progress in newsrooms, there has been much analysis of the minimal or even negative impact of programs that offer funding for newsrooms to hire Black and Brown reporters.

In a 2022 article for Harvard's Nieman Lab, staff writer Hanaa' Tameez describes how media outlets were quick to hire "diversity reporters" and "race and ethnicity reporters" in the aftermath of George Floyd's murder in 2020. She notes that roles like these are often doomed to fail because of the "lack of editorial support, lack of resources, and fundamental misunderstandings of the role journalism plays in marginalized communities."[61]

Issues like these are pervasive across the whole industry. When publishers don't provide adequate support or reduce diversity to numbers on an Excel sheet, the very reason diversity matters is undermined. The industry needs to step back to focus on that very basic question we ask ourselves at Global Press: Who's missing?

Which communities are you covering? And do your reporters have authentic access to those communities?

At Global Press, we orient our entire operation around building representative newsrooms that answer those questions. And because those questions are fundamental to our process, we know that our reporters always have authentic access to the people in their stories. The evidence-based correlation between who works in a newsroom and who is quoted in stories should be an asset, not a liability. Because when people do recognize themselves in stories and when audiences

---

61 Hanaa' Tameez, "American Journalism's 'Racial Reckoning'
    Still Has Lots of Reckoning to Do," NeimanLab, March 2022,
    accessed Febraury 3, 2023, https://www.niemanlab.org/2022/03/
    american-journalisms-racial-reckoning-still-has-lots-of-reckoning-to-do/.

everywhere read stories that include representative sourcing the results are powerful.

Building intentionally representative newsrooms is key to creating more inclusive stories. Instead of mandating a certain number of people who fit certain demographic backgrounds, the aim should be to align your audience needs with your coverage priorities. Then, it's just about finding the people with the context and the access to tell those stories. And they're out there.

Finding Partners

The pursuit of better representation in journalism doesn't have to be a complicated and expensive prospect. Undeniably, if you want to build your own bureau—as we'll discuss in a moment—it will, of course, require some significant investment. But that is just one of many ways to center local journalists.

It isn't just Global Press that has teams of journalists working in the rarely covered parts of the world. The world is literally teeming with talented local journalists who cover their communities with accuracy and sophistication each day.

Whether editors commission independent pieces, collaborate with local outlets on complex investigations, or simply republish great journalism that already exists, there are plenty of opportunities to diversify the bylines in major newspapers and websites with high-quality international journalism.

Editors can leverage an unending number of freelancer databases to find exceptional storytellers anywhere. And rather than asking the local reporter to "fix" for an outsider on their next trip, offering them the story instead is almost certain to bring new insights to your audience.

When I asked Bobby Ghosh, who is now at Bloomberg, why he thought more major publications didn't invest in local journalists around the world, he said global locations fall off the radar for legacy publications so quickly that hiring a team of local reporters directly usually doesn't make sense.

"If a big story comes up in the Maldives and we don't have someone there, it wouldn't necessarily make sense for us to invest in a relationship with somebody in the Maldives because we know by the next day, we won't care about the Maldives anymore," he said. "But if I could find an organization like Global Press that is doing great work there, then working together would be the way to go."

I think that makes a lot of sense. If providing a full-time salary for a local journalist and a translator is prohibitively expensive, there are ways to partner with other organizations that already employ local journalists—as we'll discuss below—all of which are affordable. At Global Press, for example, all of our stories are available to partners free of charge in seven languages.

Of course, this is not a foreign idea to most publishers in the United States and Europe anymore. Partnership has become a force in our industry in recent years, thanks in part to the pioneering efforts of ProPublica, a nonprofit investigative newsroom that launched in 2008. Their partnership model pushed collaboration into the mainstream, and it's time we utilized similar systems for international coverage.

Field Building

Partnerships are an excellent way to begin elevating the work of local journalists and diversifying news coverage—but ultimately, larger publications should aim to build teams of local reporters across the world. Luckily, this is not as difficult as it might at first seem.

There are thousands of journalists ready to join such teams in countries around the world. To see them, we simply have to remove some of the assumptions we've developed about this industry. Take education. We've come to see journalism as a professional career that requires advanced degrees, but it hasn't always been that way. Before someone decided that Ivy League institutions should offer master's degrees in journalism, it was an associates-degree trade at best. Peter Jennings, Walter Cronkite, and Carl Bernstein never graduated from college, so there's no reason we should assume a local journalist in Mexico who lacks a degree would struggle to thrive in the trade today.

All of these media greats were trained on the job, where the best training in journalism always happens. Journalism is not and has never been a classroom discipline. The best become the best with mentorship and hands-on experience. If that's true in New York, it's true in Ulaanbaatar too.

For this reason, field building should be a focus for all editors and publishers. We all have a stake in the longevity of our craft, so we must do what we can to train, mentor, and carefully select the journalists tasked with covering the world. And as we select those journalists, we should keep asking that same question: Who's missing?

Just as is the case in the United States, across the world the pipeline to become a journalist often runs from elite families and elite schools to prestigious publishers. Journalists across the world are often expected to have degrees in the field—which are expensive and hard to come by. They may require unpaid internships or low-paying jobs at a student newspaper, meaning those without outside assistance can't afford to become a reporter at all. And getting a shot at a journalism job often requires already knowing someone who can open the door for you.

That's why in many places a small handful of local journalists rise to international credibility while the majority labor in obscurity—if they can find work at all. Just like in all jobs, especially in publishing, once someone takes a chance on you, others are likely to do the same. In DRC, a fixer who worked with Al Jazeera for years moved on to the *Washington Post*, where he has now shared bylines with a bureau chief. He is a good journalist—very good, in fact. But he isn't one in a million. He probably isn't even one in a hundred. DRC is home to many exceptional storytellers.

So if you want unique access to these communities, you'll need to get beyond those select few and find the people no one has hired. Trust me, they are out there. When Global Press goes into a new country, we've regularly received more than a thousand applications for a handful of spots.

In some cases training may be required. In others language barriers will exist. But as we've already seen, both can be solved with simple logistics. They are not permanent roadblocks.

This process is not always easy, but it is pretty straightforward. A whole workforce of extraordinary talent awaits the international journalism industry. All we have to do is learn how to look in new places and provide an opportunity.

Local Journalists Define the Narrative

Once we have a team in place, it's Global Press policy to let our journalists take the lead. Our nonassignment policy asks them to find and tell the stories they feel most need to be told. Of course, we're not a breaking news organization, so we have some latitude there. But amazing things happen when local reporters are given the reins to write about the stories they feel most need to be told. They find extraordinary angles and ways into complex current events. And the people they find to help tell those stories differ from the publicists and the press offices issuing press releases en masse to other news outlets.

For Moky Makura, a Nigerian-born journalist with a powerful biography that includes everything from anchoring news programs to a five-year stint at the Bill and Melinda Gates Foundation, the time for narrative change is now. Today, she runs Africa No Filter, a donor collaborative focused on shifting the African narrative.

"As an industry we need to do two things: tell better stories and tell stories better," she wrote to me in an email in early 2023. "To tell better stories, we need to invest time and energy in finding stories that better represent the continent. We are not all about poverty, corruption, conflict, poor leadership, and disease. We can do with more stories that highlight the progress we are making as a continent."

At Africa No Filter, and their new news agency *Bird*, Makura is committed to building capacity for local journalists. "And not just as stringers who can bring their local contacts to a story, but ideally, as bylined authors or coauthors who bring a diversity of context to the story," she said. "What's most important now is to develop the skill set for local journalists to look for the compelling stories that are hiding in plain sight."

Whether you use partnerships or build your own teams, your aim should be to provide local journalists as much space as possible to find and tell the stories they see on the ground, while also giving them the opportunity to tell those stories without the perspective a US or European audience would normally expect.

This, on its own, would be a radical step toward better international journalism. A friend of mine in Haiti is a talented reporter who has had bylines in no fewer than five legacy US newspapers. (She asked me not to use her name to preserve her freelance relationships.) She's a bold reporter with extraordinary access and a practiced writer who can deliver copy that editors appreciate. She told me recently that no editor has ever asked her for her take on a story or an assignment. Her assignments typically come via email with a prescription for what the story will be about. Sometimes, that perspective clashes with the reality on the ground.

In cases where she's pushed back, she says it has backfired. In one instance, she was labeled "too biased" to continue covering her country because she suggested that the angles being assigned from afar were not completely accurate.

Asking a local journalist a few simple questions—What do you think? Does that track with what you're experiencing on the ground?—will inevitably enrich your publication. You'll find the stories others are missing and represent the reality in those communities far more accurately. Instead of barging in with assumptions about what people will read or forcing a narrative onto a reporter, accurate information about what is really going on in that place will finally be able to get out to a wider audience.

Protecting Your Greatest Asset

At Global Press, we've created teams of local journalists who are leading the coverage in their communities and telling stories no one else in the world is covering. And they're doing it in a way that is dignified, precise, and representative.

In 2019, 97 percent of sources quoted in Global Press stories were local people. Only 3 percent came from the NGOs and outside experts that usually dominate coverage.[62] Our journalists know how to find a story, and they know how to report it. They know how to

---

62   Global Press, 2019 Annual Report, accessed February 3, 2023, https://assets. website-files.com/60ff0792c3d63202033066be/61118a3356ed732121434dae_Global-Press_AnnualReport_2019.pdf.

balance lived experience with credentialed expertise. They know when to talk to a climate scientist and when to talk to a struggling farmer about climate change. The opportunity to work with editors, fact checkers, and translators ensures that their stories are accurate and will appeal to their local and international audiences. The freedom to find and tell these stories is the reason we're able to uncover so many stories other publications miss.

But the only way we can create room for this freedom is by keeping our journalists safe. Working with local journalists adds a new dimension of security need and newsroom responsibility.

Few in the industry are more thoughtful about these needs than Lauren Williams, CEO and cofounder of the new news organization Capital B, a local-national nonprofit news organization that centers Black voices, audience needs and experiences, and partners with the communities it serves.

"It's important that we're hiring journalists with some connection to the place they're covering," she told me in 2022. "We want our journalists to be able to build trust with the audiences. Having a stake in the story is actually an asset, rather than a hindrance to good, objective journalism."

Williams's approach to building representative newsrooms is why the organization rose to fast success. She's also mindful that being a member of the community you cover can have security implications. "It also means that the stories our journalists are working on, from violence to inequalities facing Black people, are issues the journalists and their families are dealing with too. It's difficult work."

Every publication knows how important journalist security is, but working with local journalists provides an opportunity to once again shift our thinking on what security actually means—and who should take the lead in determining what kind of security is necessary.

CHAPTER 9

Security for the Whole Journalist

Of all of the Global Press reporters around the world, Merveille Kavira Luneghe lives in the most dangerous place. She lives in Kirumba, a small town in eastern DRC, a location with over one hundred armed groups active in the area. She works tirelessly to tell stories from this place, typically distilled to a tragic dependent clause in other reporting from the country. She works tirelessly to keep herself safe too.

Merveille's continued safety is possible because Global Press has created processes that allow Merveille to take the lead on establishing her own security needs and supplements those needs with robust systems to monitor, mitigate, and respond to her ever-changing circumstances.

Since she joined Global Press in 2015, there have been times when she's requested physical security in the form of transportation to interviews. Often, this is a hired motorcyclist who drives her around so that she is not assaulted, robbed, or kidnapped. At other times, she's chosen to remove such protective measures—because moving around with visible security called too much attention to her.

In each instance that she makes a request, and that request is honored, paid for, and implemented quickly.

But security for Merveille goes beyond rides or the presence (or absence) of a bodyguard. The choice to employ a local reporter in a place like Kirumba requires investment, flexibility and trust. At one point during the early pandemic, insecurity was particularly rampant in the region. The only safe time to go out, investigate, and interview was the weekly market day. On other days, the streets were empty, making anyone outside a target. To keep Merveille safe, Global Press restructured her deadlines around this weekly reporting schedule.

The effort was more than worth it. The work she managed to produce during this difficult time was exceptional. She wrote about how fears of COVID-19 forced residents to live in fields, risking animal attack and robbery. And as violence escalated, she reported on the emergence of the opposite trend: people ignoring COVID-19 restrictions for fear of kidnapping. She also wrote about the consequences of local deforestation, a tribe losing its language, and a major local reconciliation effort.

These are stories that only Merveille could tell. And she could only tell them because we at Global Press did our job: we trusted Merveille's judgment and her knowledge of her own situation. When it came to security and stories, our answer to any request was always, yes. No matter what.

And after seven years with Global Press, Merveille trusts we will continue to support her.

"I have overcome many fears in doing this job," she told me. "Global Press provides me great support and also gives me great lattitude." The result? She can use her extraordinary talent and her profound access to tell the world stories about a place that is deeply misunderstood.

That support comes through our Duty of Care program, which is widely considered to be best in class for two reasons. First, it is built specifically for local women journalists—people for whom extraction is not an option. And second, it addresses journalist security holistically. It provides training and support services for physical, emotional, digital, and legal security needs. And it is built within an organization-wide ethos that ensures each and every journalist understands that she is more important than any story she can tell.

Often, such an approach is considered too difficult or too expensive. It is neither. In fact, it's a central part of the path forward—toward better coverage and the expansion of the role of local journalists.

A Lack of Parity

In chapter 3, I mentioned a statistic that bears repeating. If you look at the list of journalists who died on the job over the last thirty years, you will find that the overwhelming majority have been local journalists. According to the Committee to Protect Journalists, 88 percent of the journalists who have been killed since 1992 were local journalists.[63] The reasons aren't complicated. Local journalists are the least likely to have any security and often have no way out of dangerous situations. There's simply no parity between the security we offer foreign correspondents and local journalists.

"The foreign correspondent takes very different kinds of risks than a local reporter," said Bobby Ghosh, who has reported all over the world as a foreign correspondent. He has also been a local journalist

---

63   Committee to Protect Journalists, "Database of Attacks on the Press 1992-Present," cpj.com, accessed February 2, 2023, https://cpj.org/data/.

in India. "Foreign correspondents carry much less of the risk in any situation. It's not a level playing field."

The journalists who most need security in our profession are the ones who receive it least. This is, of course, not to belittle the very serious risks parachute journalists face. As I write this, the war in Ukraine rages, and exceptional parachute journalists have been providing ongoing coverage for months on end, at great personal risk and sacrifice. But those risks are constant for local journalists.

It's not just the international news outlets who don't provide adequate security. Local media houses are woefully ill equipped to offer comprehensive security solutions. That means local journalists— and the quality of their journalism—suffer.

Gamu, a senior reporter on our Zimbabwe team, says local journalists endure assault, especially in times of election, and increased media violations have become even more common since 2020.

"The proper security of journalists, which is proffered by their media organizations, is quite limited here," she told me in a 2022 conversation.

Needless to say, local journalists require more security than they are currently offered. But the plea here is not just for parity between local reporters like Gamu and a parachuter popping into town for a few days. To truly raise the quality of news coverage, we must expand our industry's definition of security for all reporters.

Duty of Care: Expanding the Concept of Security

Despite the myriad of ongoing challenges, Ghosh says he has seen an increase in recognition of the security risks local reporters face around the world.

"When I started out thirty years ago, there was no acknowledgement of the imbalance," he said. "Today I do see some degree of awareness. There are more institutions that are aware of the imbalance and are trying to rectify it. Increasingly, we see that when a local reporter gets into difficulty an international community of journalists, whether institutional or individual, rally around the cause and apply pressure on their behalf."

That is heartening and a trend that I hope continues. Yet, such efforts have not trickled down to create concrete improvements—particularly among local outlets.

"When I look at our own organization and when it comes to issues of Duty of Care, I think maybe we are four steps ahead of everyone else in terms of how [Global Press] ensures that we are safe in our coverage," Gamu told me.

Over the years, I've had many conversations with heads of security at major news organizations, and they all assure me they'd like to do more to protect the local journalists and fixers they work with. But they tell me it's too hard or too expensive. As a publisher who prioritizes safety and security above all things, I can tell you that it is neither of those things—if those things are your top priorities.

At Global Press, reporters start thinking about security before they even pitch a story. If a story requires travel, there are check-ins and travel protocols for that, which include specifying a mode of transport appropriate for the distance. Global Press covers all travel costs up front, never forcing the reporter to be reimbursed for travel expenses. Specific interviews may require more security. And postpublication security strategies are a must for sensitive stories. At the same time, online harassment protocols are prepped, as are legal responses, in the event a source threatens our reporter.

"All of this gives us leverage and minimizes risk to our lives," Gamu said. "And ultimately, Duty of Care is out there to guard us and ensure that our lives are more important than the stories we want to cover."

Global Press assembled our Duty of Care program based on this theory. Our program covers every aspect of security for our teams across the world because every reporter is entitled to physical, emotional, digital, and legal security.

Our aim is to secure the whole journalist—in every aspect of their lives—because being a good journalist requires one's whole self.

Physical Security

In 2019, Merveille wrote a story called "I Will Not Leave This Place" about why she refused to ever leave Kirumba and become a refugee. "This is a story about home," she begins. "This is the story of why so many people go. It's also the story of why I will always stay."[64]

In that story, Merveille spelled out why she loved her country, her region, and her town. She wanted to show there was more to her corner of DRC than the violence caused by armed groups and a refugee crisis, while also detailing the vast devastation such turmoil had reaped on her home in the last few decades.

It's a beautiful story, and it points to one of the challenges publishers face with local journalists. For someone like Merveille, extraction is not an option. When security in a country deteriorates, often rapidly, parachute journalists go to their embassy; they go to an airport; and they leave. That's not an option for local journalists. And even if it

---

64 Merveille Kavira Luneghe, "'I Will Not Leave This Place,'" Global Press Journal, October 2019, accessed February 3, 2023, https://globalpressjournal.com/africa/democratic-republic-of-congo/will-not-leave-place/.

were, many, like Merveille, would refuse to leave. That's where their homes are, where their babies are. Leaving just isn't a realistic option.

With extraction off the table, physical security has to focus on protecting reporters not just while reporting one difficult story but also for years after the story has been published. This requires creative solutions in which the journalist determines what they need at any particular moment to physically stay safe.

For instance, to write that story, Merveille requested a drone. She wanted to take aerial photos of her region to show its beauty. But there was a real risk sending a drone around areas with numerous active armed groups. To avoid any potential conflict, she took the drone to some village chiefs and leaders of armed groups in the area and let them see it. She even let them fly it. It was her way of getting community buy-in and showing them that her work wasn't a threat. That kept her, her crew, and her local community safe while she reported that story.

Only Merveille would have known how best to approach that situation, and that's usually the case. Local journalists are the best judges of their own circumstances and what they need to do to stay safe. They know their context. They know the local threats and the assumptions people in their community will make.

Letting local journalists take the lead on physical security can even improve coverage. In 2022, one of Global Press's best reporters, Linda Mujuru in Zimbabwe, published a piece in her ongoing coverage of the use of mercury in gold mining in Zimbabwe.

Linda had spent years covering the unfolding story and had strong connections with the miners who handled mercury daily. After weeks in the field with miners and community members, her more challenging source was a government official in the Ministry of Mines and Mining Development.

Linda got the runaround for weeks while trying to get this interview. She knew she needed more than a simple "no comment." When she was finally granted a meeting, he began the meeting by saying: "I don't like journalists."

Clearly, this was a tense moment. She was sitting down with a powerful man in a government that had a history of repressing journalism. But because Linda was in a position to judge her own security, she was able to calm the situation and explain her story. She told the official that she understood the nuances and challenges the government faced—banning mercury overnight would plunge five hundred thousand people who rely on it into abject poverty. She took the time to earn his trust. And as a result, he gave a forthcoming, on-camera interview that was rare and powerful for a government official in Zimbabwe.

Her approach was a far cry from the smash-and-grab interview style that parachute reporters are notorious for using. Often, government interviews are saved for the last day of an assignment. On the way out of town, the parachuter does an aggressive "American-style" grilling of an official that is antagonistic and culturally inappropriate. The result? The parachuter gets footage of the African official getting angry on camera or walking out of the interview. From there, it's easy to lean into stereotypes, suggesting to audiences that he has something to hide or is unfriendly to journalists. But often the truth lies somewhere in the middle, and these aggressive techniques fail to yield any insight, all while leaving the local team supporting the parachuter in danger afterward.

In contrast, Linda was able to perform a masterclass interview that produced real insight for viewers. Linda's story was featured on *PBS NewsHour*, Quartz Africa, and other local outlets. That day, I was so proud of Linda and the team that worked tirelessly on this story.

But I was also happy to see a Zimbabwean official treated fairly and speaking freely on a difficult and nuanced topic for the world to see.

This interview was much more reflective of what governance in many parts of Africa actually looks like. There is undeniable corruption—and in some places, violence—but there are also people trying to do the best they can with limited resources to make their countries better.

As the story's publication date approached, we asked Linda if she felt safe. She did. She said giving the government ample opportunity to respond as she had would protect her. And she was right.

There's clear value, then, in adjusting mindsets on physical security, but to be truly holistic, we also have to expand this adjustment into areas of security policy that currently seem effective. As I mentioned in chapter 3, HEFAT training is a popular, and I believe usually ineffective, form of training for journalists. It typically involves group scenario-based training, often provided by military veterans. These veterans will simulate kidnappings, car accidents, hostile negotiations, and mass casualty events. News organizations pay these training organizations to simulate holding their journalists at gunpoint and to show them what to do if a grenade goes off.

This is a theory of security built on preparing for the rare worst-case scenarios, and in my experience, it usually does more harm than good. Global Press used to offer HEFAT training for team members preparing to go overseas to train or conduct workshops. But after more than one team member reported trauma resurgence, increased anxiety, and other symptoms, including insomnia, we knew we had to find a better way.

There may be a place for this type of preparation, but suggesting to a journalist preparing to travel abroad that the people "over there" are likely to kidnap, assault, or murder them hardly bodes well for escaping stereotypical narratives when the reporter arrives.

The simple alternative is to focus on preparing journalists for the risks they are most likely to face. While specific circumstances differ, the truth is that most risks a journalist faces can be forecasted—and thus also mitigated.

In 2017, Global Press did a survey of three hundred journalists across East Africa, and we found that the number one risk these journalists faced wasn't rape, grenades, or muggings. The answer that topped the list was injuries to the palms of their hands from falling off the back of boda bodas, or motorcycle taxis.

That's not to say those more serious security risks aren't important or don't happen—nor that some training for these scenarios isn't valuable—only that we should work to secure our reporters daily, not just in worst case scenarios. And that includes acknowledging the mental and emotional toll the job can take.

Emotional Security

In 2020, Anthony Feinstein, a professor of psychiatry at the University of Toronto, gave a speech at the Reuters Institute about his twenty years of research on the emotional well-being of journalists.[65]

He began his remarks with a story of a Canadian reporter who had covered conflict in East Africa. After she had a mental breakdown and went home, she found her way to his clinic. He asked her why she had not reached out for help earlier, and he said she replied: "You don't understand my profession. If I had told my manager I was feeling this

---

65 Anthony Feinstein, "I've Studied Journalists under Pressure for 20 Years. Here's What I've Learned So Far," Reuters Institute for the Study of Journalism, June 2020, accessed February 3, 2023, https://reutersinstitute.politics.ox.ac.uk/news/ive-studied-journalists-under-pressure-20-years-heres-what-ive-learned-so-far.

way, they would not have sent me out into the field again, and my career as a frontline correspondent would have been over."

Her fears are not uncommon.

According to a 2016 report from the Dart Center for Journalism and Trauma at Columbia University, 80 to 100 percent of journalists have experienced a work-related traumatic event.[66] Anxiety, depression, post-traumatic stress, and insomnia are common.

For far too long, the assumption has been that those who suffered mental health issues simply lack the character profile for journalism. I use "character" intentionally because we have a very Hollywoodized conceptualization of journalists—dare devils almost eager to put their lives in danger day after day.

But this image doesn't correspond to reality. We might assume that someone becomes a reporter because they have a natural appetite for risk, but that is not the case. What motivates most reporters centers more around concepts of justice. Risk is often an undesirable outcome.

The pandemic forced a bit of a reckoning with this, but support systems and structures are inconsistently applied across newsrooms.

A recent *Reuters* study tells us that three-quarters of women journalists reported suffering serious psychological impact from the pandemic. In another sampling of journalists in 2020, 70 percent said they suffered psychological distress during the same period. According to the same study, 26 percent have "clinically significant anxiety."[67]

---

66   River Smith, Elana Newman, Susan Drevo, and Autumn Slaughter, "Covering Trauma: Impact on Journalists," Dart Center for Journalism & Trauma, July 2015, accessed February 2, 2023, https://dartcenter.org/content/covering-trauma-impact-on-journalists.

67   Jonas Osmann, Meera Selva, and Anthony Feinstein, "How Have Journalists Been Affected Psychologically by Their Coverage of the COVID-19 Pandemic? A Descriptive Study of Two International News Organisations," National Library of Medicine, July 2021, accessed February 3, 2023, DOI: 10.1136/bmjopen-2020-045675.

Many of the people included in these figures have burned out on journalism entirely. We've seen a mass exodus of journalists from the field after the pandemic—and that isn't only due to cuts on the publisher side. Many journalists have chosen to find less emotionally taxing work. Others have stepped away temporarily for their mental health.

Ed Yong at *The Atlantic* recently announced he was taking a six-month sabbatical from reporting after nearly three years covering COVID-19. He mentioned in his Twitter post announcing his decision that his coverage of the pandemic had "deeply broken me."[68]

That same stress is at work on local journalists covering war, violence, and corruption across the world. Because of how we cover international news, local journalists are most commonly hired to cover the most horrific events. Where other journalists can cover a community more holistically, there's little room for coverage of the arts, technology, business, or family in those places in our current model. That means reporting on violence on the frontlines becomes the status quo. And unlike Yong, local journalists almost certainly don't have employers willing to give them the time or resources to recover. As a freelancer or a fixer, the low pay, the total lack of benefits, and the lack of job security means there's no room for emotional support.

All of which is to say that mental health security is extremely important for all reporters—but especially local journalists.

It is possible to break this cycle.

"Creating policies around Duty of Care is important," says Global Press COO Laxmi Parthasarathy. "But creating an ethos of Duty of Care that allows and encourages people to talk about their challenges openly and then get services in response is the key."

---

68   Ed Yong, Twitter post, September 30, 2022, 9:21 a.m., https://twitter.com/edyong209/status/1575838235129180160.

For news leaders, understanding the scope of the challenges team members are facing is the first step in designing adequate care options for them.

The second step is recognizing that, as with physical security, emotional security may look different for journalists in different locations. In 2016, we launched the Global Press Wellness Network, which which offers our reporters access to licensed mental health professionals who speak their languages. The network allows for unlimited long or short-term counseling sessions. Reporters can request sessions through a system that conceals their identity from their editors and colleagues. When they put a request in, they're matched with a counselor within twenty-four hours.

This important service isn't utilized equally across the world. Uptake often follows patterns within communities. Argentina, for example, has the highest number of psychologists per capita. Argentinian culture sees therapy as an important and positive undertaking. The same is largely true in Mexico.

"But in Zimbabwe, there is only one psychiatrist in the whole country," Meagan Demitz, Global Press's Wellness Network manager told me. "And in Mongolia individual therapy is a different story. People are much more likely to attend group psychoeducation workshops than individual sessions with a counselor."

This is why our wellness network doesn't seek to force the same solution on everyone. We know that isn't just unhelpful, it can have serious consequences. In the book *Crazy Like Us*, author Ethan Watters details the actions of US counselors who went over to Sri Lanka to provide mental health support to those who survived the 2004 tsunami.[69] In sessions, the US therapists encouraged the use of

---

69   Ethan Watters, *Crazy Like Us: The Globalization of the American Psyche* (New York City: Free Press, 2010).

talk therapy to process trauma. They found the local people extremely resistant. No matter the trauma they had experienced, local people simply didn't want to participate. Those therapists assumed their Sri Lankan patients must be in denial or shock. What the therapists didn't recognize was that the Sri Lankans they were treating had Buddhist beliefs and cultural norms that gave meaning to those horrible events. They were processing trauma, just in a different way. Watters concludes that abeling them as traumatized could have been more traumatizing than leaving them alone.

To provide comprehensive mental health security, then, you have to do more than create an opening for discussion and the opportunity for therapy—you have to pair it with solutions that meet the needs of your people based on their personal and cultural circumstances. At Global Press, group psychoeducation classes on key topics have become increasingly popular in places where individual counseling uptake has been minimal. And where that isn't sufficient, editors keep an eye out for burnout after a reporter routinely covers difficult stories. They are quick to suggest a break for alternate topics. Flexible leave policies help too.

Perhaps the single most important step publishers can take in this area is creating the space for honest expectations and clear limitations of individual journalists. Global Press opened a bureau in Puerto Rico in 2018. After providing a three-day Duty of Care training for our new team members, I offered a two-day version for Puerto Rican journalists working in other newsrooms throughout the capital.

After Hurricane Maria hit Puerto Rico in 2017, mental health among journalists was known to be frayed. In the training, I heard stories that could only be described as unrelentingly traumatic. This trauma was compounded by newsrooms that forced journalists to get the story at all costs. When a disaster strikes, local journalists are expected to cope with personal loss, anxiety, and trauma and cover the events, often for long periods of time—and the circumstances in Puerto Rico were no different. One man broke down as he recounted missing his mother's funeral because he was not allowed to leave his post on the other side of the island. Several in the group said they experienced extreme anxiety symptoms at the sounds of wind or rain. And they all said they had no choice but to continue because they needed the jobs.

In such circumstances, the worst of these emotional consequences could have been avoided if news leaders had provided more clarity about what was required and also provided more accommodation— particularly for those at greatest risk of anxiety.

When Global Press leaders consult with other newsrooms on their security policies, we always recommend a risk profile assessment for reporters. This assessment should be paired with a clear articulation of the news organization's own risk appetite. Journalists tend to have one of four risk profiles, which we describe as Aggressive, Moderate Conservative, Casual. It's important for the journalist to know if the work will place particular strain on them, and it's equally important for editors to make conscientious choices about which reporter ends up on a story. Putting a conservative reporter on the frontlines of a violent protest is likely to create intense anxiety for that reporter. And notably, it may not yield the type of story the publisher is hoping for. Giving an aggressive reporter carte blanche to cover a potentially dangerous or chaotic situation as they see fit will likely not pan out either. Aggressive reporters tend to act first and think later, which often results in finding themselves in hot water with no escape plan.

In Mexico, Global Press reporter Mar Garcia says she has a very conservative risk profile. She's not interested in covering protests or violence or corruption. At Global Press she's been allowed to develop her own areas of expertise, in a manner that suits her risk profile and her physical and emotional needs. The results have been extraordinary.

"I cover art and beauty in Mexico," she told me. "I'm passionate about telling people these stories so they better understand my place."

Mar's Mexico is truly magical. She reminds us that even the most challenging places deserve comprehensive coverage. Mexico is more than cartels and a border wall. Readers recognize this every time she takes them with her into a museum or inside a family's home as they prepare for Dia de Muertos celebrations.

The simple act of taking part in a thirty-minute risk profile exercise lets a journalist know the organization cares about their well-being and also increases the likelihood of long-term, high-quality coverage by putting the right reporter on the right stories.

That's not to say that conservative reporters can't or shouldn't cover difficult stories—but they need a plan in place to ensure their success. That plan should likely include support resources during and after the story has been reported.

Digital Security

Laptops get stolen all the time. It's a hazard for any profession, but for reporters, it can be more serious. If a reporter's computer is stolen while she's logged into her email or work systems, source information may also be in jeopardy. In cases like these, it's easy to see why a holistic approach to security is necessary. A physical security emergency, like getting robbed, can quickly turn into a digital security emergency. And the emotional consequences of robbery or the anxiety about source safety all add up.

We live in a digital world. For that reason, every journalist everywhere needs digital security training. They need to know how to manage passwords and social media accounts. They need tools to make sure personal information is not readily available online.

But digital security needs to go still further. One of the major issues that journalists face today is online harassment. Harassment can lead to mental and physical security risks, so giving journalists the resources to reduce harassment, and to know how to respond, has to be central to any security program.

A recent study from the International Women's Media Foundation revealed that 70 percent of women in journalism report online harassment.[70] In 2022, Global Press faced it across a wide variety of fronts. A reporter in Uganda, for example, received dozens of calls and emails from an unhappy source. That escalated into fears of being followed and threats to her physical safety.

The consequences of failing to address digital security needs can be extreme. In fact, it can lead to a loss of coverage entirely.

In Sri Lanka, for example, the vast majority of media is centered in Colombo, the country's largest city, and available in Sinhala, the language of the country's majority group. According to a 2022 report by the press freedom watchdog group Reporters Without Borders, "The Sri Lankan press is directed mainly to the Sinhalese and Buddhist majority, who make up three-quarters of the population. Open criticism of the Buddhist religion or its clergy is very dangerous. As a rule, treating issues involving the Tamil minority and/or Muslims is considered extremely sensitive. Journalists and media who risked it

---

70   International Women's Media Foundation, "Online Violence and Harassment," iwmf.org, accessed February 2, 2023, https://www.iwmf.org/programs/online-harassment/#:~:text=The%20IWMF%20and%20Trollbusters'%20Attacks,profession%20due%20to%20online%20attacks..

in recent years have been targeted by arrests, death threats, or coordinated cyber-attacks."[71]

Global Press first trained a small cohort of journalists in Sri Lanka in 2009. We added a few members to our team in 2013, all in and around Colombo. As Global Press grew, we became better able to push into more remote areas to recruit even more diverse women journalists to our team. In 2018, led by Manori Wijesekera, whom you met in chapter 1, we began recruitment in the country's north, which is home to the majority of the country's Tamil population and was the site of the country's brutal civil war.

We successfully hired a bold team of Tamil women in Jaffna and Mannar, locations with scant local or international coverage. But our recruitment efforts missed a significant population we were hoping to attract: not a single Muslim woman applied for the role, despite significant on-the-ground outreach.

"Within the Muslim community, there is a distrust of media and how media companies in Sri Lanka operate," Manori said. "Media are seen as misrepresenting the Muslim community, disparaging them, and even demonizing them."

Today, more than a decade after the civil war ended, there is still no strong Muslim media company in Sri Lanka.

Manori says local Muslim women didn't join for a more personal reason too.

"In 2018, I met more than a dozen Muslim women who were eager to hear about Global Press. Two of them were teachers and talked about many of their former students who would thrive as GP reporters. But not a single one applied," Manori recalled in a 2022 conversation.

---

71 Reporters Without Borders, "Sri Lanka, 2022," accessed February 3, 2023, https://rsf. org/en/country/sri-lanka.

Why?

"Hate speech on social media against the few Muslim journalists in Sri Lanka has also led Muslim families to consider journalism as unsafe and unsuitable for women in their families," she said. "When a community has not consumed ethical, accurate media it is incredibly hard to be convinced that it can be done. It takes a leap of faith."

Legal Security

Most news organizations have in-house counsel or legal support on retainer. But too few offer legal protection to local reporters in jurisdictions around the world.

When a sensitive story could face legal backlash, a lawyer is brought in to make sure the paper or news channel is on sure footing. But if you're going to work with local journalists, you have to expand the legal protection you're offering. If you ask a US lawyer to review a piece, they might tell you that there are no legal concerns—for you. Their job is to see if there's a potential issue according to US law that might affect the publication and the journalists within US borders.

But that's only helpful for the people within those borders. It doesn't protect journalists outside the country.

Right now, for example, Merveille is doing a story on Congolese rappers who keep getting thrown in jail. These rappers are advocating for peace, but they are technically being accused of violating two new laws, one on insulting the head of state and the other on demoralizing the army. And writing about them could be risky for her.

A lawyer in the United States would say there are no concerns with this story, and that is absolutely true for Global Press, a US-based publication. But that lawyer can't tell us whether Merveille is at risk legally in the country and province where she lives.

For that, she needs a Congolese lawyer who knows Congolese law. And that resource has to be available for every local journalist. Like mental health and digital security, lawyers may not be needed every day, but they have to be available when the need arises to provide the most locally relevant support.

Redlines

When we consult with other news organizations on how to improve their holistic Duty of Care practices, one of my first questions is always "What are your redlines?"

Without fail, newsroom leaders hate this question. Journalism is an industry of free-speech activists, truth-telling zealots, and often, stubborn idealists. They don't want their scopes limited or lines drawn around the work they can do.

But redlines are important. Redlines, I frequently argue, are one way that a news organization can communicate to its employees the parameters of their safety.

At Global Press, for example, we won't open a news bureau in a country where libel is punishable by death. We've never been sued for libel. But it's a risk I'm unwilling to take, especially when truth isn't a defense against libel in too many places.

Redlines help to create strong, unwavering policies and guidelines for newsroom team members. Redlines also help to unite the whole team so that each person is able to uphold the Duty of Care.

The absence of these clear boundaries and crisp decision-making protocols can be devastating.

On July 16, 2021, Danish Siddiqui, an Indian photojournalist with Reuters, was killed while he was embedded with troops in Afghanistan. In a Reuters investigation into his death published by the news organization in August of that year, it was revealed that Siddiqui's convoy was also attacked three days earlier, yet he was allowed to stay.[72]

At Reuters, an organization known for robust security measures, editors and managers have responsibility for approving or rejecting risky assignments and have the authority to end them. Journalists, too, have the option of withdrawing from the field. But in the wake of his death some journalists inside Reuters began questioning the security protocol and the decision-making strategy that allowed him to stay embedded after the first attack. According to a report prepared and edited by Reuters journalists who weren't involved in managing the assignment, "editors in South Asia weren't part of the decision to embed Siddiqui with Afghan commandos and also had no advance notice of the Spin Boldak mission," where he was eventually killed.[73]

It was initially reported that he was killed in crossfire, but later revealed that he died after being left behind by the convoy he was embedded with. He was shot multiple times after he died and his body was mutilated by the Taliban, according to the Reuters investigation.

His death was a tragedy. And, of course, the risks of this kind of assignment were well-known, and were deeply understood by Siddiqui himself. But the fact that questions swirl about the decision-making strategy—who was in the know and other basic questions—makes the conversation about redlines even more important.

If the process had been crystal clear, he may have still died. Redlines aren't bulletproof, but consistent, comprehensive security policy is any news organization's best chance to avoid tragedy.

---

72   Stephen Grey, Charlotte Greenfield, Devjyot Ghoshal, Alasdair Pal, and Reade Levinson, "Reuters Photographer Was Killed after Being Left Behind in Retreat, Afghan General Says," Reuters, August 2021, accessed February 3, 2023, https://www.reuters.com/investigates/special-report/afghanistan-conflict-reuters-siddiqui.

73   Ibid.

Redlines are most important when the reporter is in the field and before the piece has been published. Those are the moments in which the news organization has the most control over the well-being of its reporter. Once released, a plethora of digital, legal, and emotional security risks emerge.

Still, the vast majority of risks journalists face can be anticipated. The opportunity to get ahead of digital harassment, ensure legal support, and safeguard the reporter's physical and mental health are there, and it's easier to provide that security when you prepare for risks beforehand.

Five Essentials

There is a perception that all journalist security is prohibitively expensive. But in truth, the status quo is far more expensive. Our industry's lack of emphasis on Duty of Care is costing people their health, and it's costing news organizations their best talent.

This profession, this work, is always going to carry risk. So, instead of dwelling on the cost of security, let us collectively refocus our time and energies on mitigating that risk.

We can do that by focusing on five simple things that can greatly bolster the physical security of journalists everywhere: cash, protective gear, safe modes of transport, the ability to opt out, and most importantly, foresight.

Cash

Ensuring journalists have cash on hand is one of the simplest recommendations we make to newsroom partners who come to Global Press News Services, the B2B consulting division of Global Press.

Reconsidering travel and reimbursement policies for reporters, especially reporters who are traveling or based overseas, can be a lifesaver. In 2021 as Kabul fell to the Taliban, many NGOs and news organizations reached out to Global Press for advice on how to keep their local freelancers safe. In truth, by the time they reached out, there was little risk mitigation possible; the situation had already progressed to a point that required crisis response. A month prior, though, as the Taliban began to take city after city, would have been a great time to advance freelance payments and to front staffers the coming month's (or three month's) salary.

Protective Gear

We often think about protective gear in terms of fancy SUVs or helmets and flak jackets. But outside of a war zone, the most essential proactive gear can be the least expensive, like a first aid kit or a solar-powered charger.

But even in a war zone, reporters might not have what they need. In May of 2022, as the war in Ukraine escalated, the Rory Peck Trust, a UK-based nonprofit media organization that works to ensure the safety of freelance journalists, sent out a plea for protective gear.[74] Between February, when the war started, and May, at least twelve journalists were killed, and many more were injured while on assignment.

Sourcing and accessing essential protective equipment, including first aid kits, was extremely challenging. "Very early on in the crisis, the requests we were receiving indicated that one of the biggest needs of journalists was protective equipment," Johanna Pisco, programmes

---

74   Patrick Egwu, "Journalists Must Be Protected at All Costs. They Are in Ukraine to Keep Us Informed," Reuters Institute for the Study of Journalism, May 2022, accessed February 3, 2023, https://reutersinstitute.politics.ox.ac.uk/news/journalists-must-be-protected-all-costs-they-are-ukraine-keep-us-informed.

manager at Rory Peck Trust, wrote in a fundraising plea.[75] "These are mostly freelance journalists, and we know that it is that group who most times don't have access to the resources that staff journalists would have access to, including safety gear and kits."

Safe Transport

In our survey of journalists in East Africa, the number one way most reporters told us they had been hurt while reporting was in boda boda, or motorcycle taxi, accidents.

Boda bodas are fast and efficient. They are also extremely dangerous, especially over long distances. Designing safe transport policies that account for who is traveling, the distance being traveled, and the time of travel is essential.

Safe transport options paired with efficient check in policies can be a lifesaver. At Global Press, reporters who travel within their country for stories must provide contact information for the driver; evidence of backup fuel and spare tires; or bus numbers and a photo of the bus's license plate number. Depending on the distance being traveled, the anticipated danger along the way, and any additional dangers posed by the type of story being covered, a check in schedule is set, from once a day in the evening for a typical story, all the way to hourly for riskier ones. Simple SMS messages or GPS pin drops can confirm a reporter is safe and on track. A missed check in allows us to start our search or inquiry from a recent last known location, rather than the start of the reporter's journey.

I'm often asked if reporters are annoyed by policies like this. In general, the answer is no, because the policies are reinforced by the

---

75   Ibid.

ethos of Duty of Care, which says, "We have your back; we're in this together."

The Ability to Opt Out

For people outside the news industry, this one seems like a given. For people on the inside we know it's anything but. The chances that a reporter wants to walk away from a story, especially a big one, are slim. The chances that a news organization will be supportive of that choice are even slimmer.

And the truth is that stories you walk away from hurt. As I write this paragraph I have six stories whizzing through my mind, stories that were never told because the dangers mounted, and the risk was too great. In each of these six cases, the dangers at hand were different. One case involved the threat of an authoritarian regime. We considered giving the story to an international partner so it could see the light of day, but then we thought better of it. It would be apparent that it came from our reporter. So, we let it go. In another case, after reporting on a conflict between two communities for years, the reporter had to opt out for her own mental health.

The pain and the frustration of the untold stories are not insignificant. But the life and the health of the reporter is more important. Protecting those leaves room for the possibility that the reporter can tell the story another day, in a different way.

Foresight

Most importantly, newsroom leaders, editors, colleagues, and reporters themselves can mitigate the vast majority of risks they face with foresight.

The risks journalists encounter are mostly predictable. New ones will emerge as digital sophistication and authoritarian angst create new pathways for harassment and punishment, but for the most part, the risk list is known.

It's no secret that human beings do their best thinking and planning outside of moments of crisis. So taking the time to draft a risk playbook so that newsroom leadership and reporters know what to do in a given moment can not only save lives, but it can also boost newsroom morale and improve coverage.

"Duty of Care is everything," Laxmi told me. "It's not a separate program that sits to one side; it's in everything. And our team needs to be able to feel it everywhere. From leave policies and insurance benefits to check in protocols and risk assessments. It's alive in everything and everyone is responsible for making it work."

And paying for Duty of Care can be feasible for any news organization. At Global Press, which is about a $6 million-per-year nonprofit organization, we add a 3 percent Duty of Care line to each and every grant. This way, each philanthropic partner shares the cost of the programming, the gear, and the benefits that help to keep our reporters safe.

Noella Nyirabihogo, whom we met in chapter 6, has been with Global Press in DRC for more than a decade. She became so passionate about Duty of Care that she trained to become a first aid trainer, and taught her colleagues across three countries the basics of emergency first aid. Unlike HEFAT training, Noella's class didn't focus on gunshot wounds or kidnapping. She taught her colleagues how to dress their own wounds and to care for themselves in the most commonly faced situations.

Today, Noella is Global Press's Duty of Care liaison for Africa. For her and her dozens of colleagues around the world, Duty of Care is more than a program, it's a reason to stay at Global Press.

"I know other journalists who go out into the field, and they have to bring the news back, no matter what. No one really cares about what they are going through, about their safety," she says. "There is no department in charge of evaluating their potential risks or options for their emotional security. I mean, no one really cares about that aspect of their job."

At Global Press, Noella knows her safety is our top priority.

CHAPTER 10

Doing It Differently

Fixing the news has felt like an intractable problem for so long. But the road to a prosperous, trustworthy, respected journalism industry is not as impassable as many assume. There is a clear path forward and a role for each of us to play along the way.

The news is not alone in facing a seemingly existential crisis. As a global society, we have many serious and complex problems in front of us that we must resolve. And in each case, both individually and collectively, we have found ways to do our part to make things better.

We all know, for example, that our warming planet is a potentially catastrophic problem. While the solution to climate change will likely be found at the international policy level, that doesn't stop companies from reducing emissions or the rest of us from remembering to turn off our lights. The willingness to enact change individually is particularly high on this issue. A 2021 Pew-CNBC study found that

80 percent of people were willing to change their behavior to help fight climate change.[76]

Together, we need to embrace similarly simple changes to reimagine international journalism.

Unlike climate change, this is a problem that regular people can fix. One person driving an electric vehicle may not reduce our carbon emissions much, but one particularly active news consumer can start holding a publication to account. Within the industry, each of us is in charge of how we practice our craft. In other words, one reader, one journalist, or one editor can make a huge difference in updating the news model to meet the needs of our present moment.

Throughout this book, I hope I have articulated the reasons international news is in this predicament. We are failing to tell dignified and precise stories about places around the world that don't match old definitions of "important." We are focusing on disaster and sensationalism instead of accuracy. We're overusing fixers without giving them credit or the authority to tell their own stories. And we aren't keeping our journalists as secure as they deserve to be.

But as I have said throughout, these are not unresolvable issues. And this is our moment to step up, put the effort in, and reimagine international journalism.

The world is ready for the fuller story. Local reporters have already proven that they are equal to the task.

Now is the time for each of us to do our part to elevate them to the byline.

---

76 Catherine Clifford, "More Than 80% Say They'd Change Their Behavior to Fight Climate Change, but U.S. Conservatives Lag," CNBC, September 2021, accessed February 3, 2023, https://www.cnbc.com/2021/09/14/climate-change-to-change-behavior-80percent-of-respondents-tell-pew.html.

Readers

In Global Press's US audience research so many people said that the news felt like a black box.[77] The inner workings seemed completely inscrutable, and readers felt powerless to do anything about improving the quality of output.

But that doesn't have to be the case. News consumers have more power in this relationship than they believe, and they should feel emboldened to ask questions and hold news publications accountable.

Say Something

Often, when readers see low-quality reporting their first instinct is to tune out or turn the page. But going forward, readers will have to take a more active role in their news consumption. If you see a pattern of poor reporting or read an article that doesn't pass the smell test, say something.

This doesn't have to be particularly time consuming, and it definitely should not be confused with just complaining or stooping to online harassment of journalists you might not like. I'm talking about asking questions about process and premises and calling out inaccuracies and a lack of representative sourcing. Holding news organizations to account doesn't take much time to yield incredible results.

In August of 2021, a man named Michael Stoler wrote a letter to Kelly McBride, the public editor of NPR—the person responsible for

---

77   Lexmi Parthasarathy and Cristi Hegranes, "Unlocking U.S. Audience Demand for International News," Media Impact Funders, February 2023, accessed February 31, 2023, https://bit.ly/globalpressaudience.

acting as a liaison between the public and a news organization, often responding to questions of ethics and accuracy.[78] He wrote:

"Hello, I really wish NPR reporters would stop using the term 'mud huts.' I'm not sure what it means. I don't see how one can make a hut out of mud. Do they mean a sort of adobe, used in many places throughout the world, or brick? The reporters seem to use the term to describe the dwellings of people in developing countries, and it suggests the most primitive sort of shelter, in a condescending, even demeaning way. Would they describe the citizens of trendy Santa Fe as living in 'mud huts'?"

McBride investigated his request, searching for NPR's recent usage of the term, and reached out to a variety of language experts, including me, to get our take on Stoler's claims.

My response was emphatic: Stoler was right. In an interview for her newsletter I said that when a journalist uses that term, they are "describing either an impoverished area or an area that lacks infrastructure, without actually saying that."[79] The term mud huts implies poverty without proving it. International journalism is filled with such imprecise words that lead readers to the assumption of poverty.

Stoler's simple act of writing a few sentences caused a whole news organization to evaluate its word choice. That's a powerful act of change, all thanks to a single news consumer who spent a few minutes responding to a style point he knew was wrong.

This isn't an isolated example. Look closely, and individual readers and viewers are already beginning to hold media organizations to account. Some of the stories in this book were only possible because of news consumers. Remember Shilu's story about the little girl who

---

78   NPR, "When You Hear the Term 'Mud Huts' What Image Comes to Mind?," NPR, September 2022, accessed February 3, 2023, https://www.npr.org/sections/publiceditor/2022/09/23/1124697740/when-you-hear-the-term-mud-huts.

79   Ibid.

didn't receive brain surgery in Nepal? That story came from a viewer who spoke up and made Global Press aware of the inaccuracy.

These are not minor changes. They're crucial adjustments if we want to reform the current model for international coverage.

Master Media Literacy

Anyone can read the news. But too few people have the skills to truly assess a piece of journalism.

One of my favorite things about teaching at Georgetown has been watching my students become whip-smart news consumers. In one exercise, I asked students to analyze ten stories from Africa published by the *Washington Post*, in an attempt to identify the publication's strategy for covering the continent. They quickly homed in on a hodgepodge of bylines from reporters based all over the world. They noticed poor sourcing practices, like stories entirely built on second-hand online sources. They flagged when datelines were thousands of miles from the action and when stories contained official voices but no local people. The most industrious students did LinkedIn searches for all of the sources in stories to understand if they were truly representative. In one case, 100 percent of the sources in a story were white, and none were currently living in Africa. And they grimaced when they saw stereotypical storylines cobbled together with victim-centered language.

In a matter of a single semester, they went from news skimmers to hawk-eyed readers.

Learning to be an attentive, equity-minded reader helps news consumers get more out of the great stories, and it helps them hold the lesser stories to account. It helps clarify why proximity is king, the importance of equitable sourcing, and when it's time to start asking questions of journalists and publications.

Journalists

I know many burned-out journalists who say changing standards and practices in their newsroom just feels impossible. They don't control style guides or approve budgets. They are stuck in the grind.

I hear that. But in most newsrooms, there are still small yet significant ways journalists can advocate for more equitable international news practices that can increase trust in all reporting.

One of the most powerful things a journalist can do is find opportune times to share their platform.

If not for David Folkenflik of NPR, for instance, CNN would probably never have corrected their story about little Salina. After months of reporting, we still needed Gupta's side of the story. CNN provided a general comment but refused us access to Gupta.

That's when I reached out to Folkenflik, a well-known and reputable media critic. After I shared Shilu's story and all of the reporting, photos, and fact checking that went with it, he agreed to do a follow up story that would publish just hours after ours—helping to spread the story to a much wider audience. Most importantly, though, he was able to get on the phone with Gupta.

"Thanks to you and your willingness to share anything I asked for—and your willingness to talk through what had occurred—I had a lot of information. I was able to talk, at some length, to Dr. Gupta himself," Folkenflik recalled when we spoke about the story again in 2022.

When I asked Folkenflik to reflect on the experience all those years ago, he said: "I wish they had engaged with you. It may be that they felt they finally had to once NPR was paying attention, and because reputationally, Gupta cares about what his peers see and hear."

Folkenflik is right. While the system still provides more power to voices at large and legacy media outlets, journalists at such institutions can make or break many stories reported by their local colleagues. Sometimes, all it takes to elevate a story is to use that authority to get answers or attract eyeballs.

Be a Good Partner

Making a big phone call or following up on local reporting is only one way journalists can contribute. Another, and one of the best, is for journalists to simply give credit where it is due. Ideally, this may look like sharing, or even passing on a story to give the byline to a local journalist. In many cases, though, it can simply involve transparently describing your reporting process in the body of your story. If you use translators, say so—and name them. Readers deserve to know which quotes were translated and by whom.

It takes a lot of work to report international stories. Parachute journalists work with fixers who do much of the research and reporting—as well as much of the writing sometimes. It costs nothing to share this fact with your readers. If your fixer wrote the first draft of the story, give them a shared byline. And advocate for their day rate, acknowledging as the foreign reporters in this book have, that they are essential to the process.

These transparent descriptions, mentions, credits, and bylines go a long way to building the authority of local journalists so they can report their own stories.

Watch Your Language

Word choice reinforces worldview. That means journalists have tremendous power to influence the way people understand the world.

International media is replete with euphemisms, imprecise phrases that imply poverty, limit agency, and lead readers to make assumptions about people and places.

When we use terms like "Global South," the purpose is less geographic than as a sanitized synonym for poverty. Such terms signal to our readers that understanding the place in question isn't important because it doesn't deserve precise recognition. Billions of people across multiple continents can all be swept together as poor and of less consequence with the use of that phrase. Similarly, using phrases like "ethnic tension" tell readers that they don't need to trouble themselves with the specifics; it's just another story about people "over there" killing each other.

Using words and phrases like these encourage people to make assumptions and reinforce stereotypes. And there's no added value in them. They're frustrating to readers because they are sweeping and poorly defined. In our audience research, no participant could correctly define the phrase Global South. In the absence of a definition, people had vast assumptions about what it meant and what it signaled about the people who live "there."

As journalists, we can always aim for more precise word choices. We can strengthen our mental muscle that allows us to recognize when we're using poorly considered language. We can flex that muscle to sense when we are using descriptive details about people overseas that we'd never use at home, like defining a professional woman by the number of children she has.

One of the best tricks to improve dignity in writing is to avoid labels. Victim, survivor, inmate, immigrant: Each of these words carries a heavy weight of associations, assumptions, and prejudices. By pivoting to describing people's actions rather than identity, we can better ensure that the source is described in dignified terms, in ways that would allow them to recognize themselves in the story.

Newsroom Leaders

People in the United States know very little about Mongolia—and with some good reason. Because it's remote and one of the least populated countries in the world, it's safe to say that Mongolia rarely makes the evening news.

But when newsroom leaders make an effort to connect global events for their audiences, often by leveraging the work of local reporters, extraordinary things can happen. Even rural, remote Mongolia can seem relevant.

In June 2021, Khorloo Khukhnokhoi, a Global Press reporter in Mongolia, began investigating virginity testing in high schools around the country. This horrific practice—and its ubiquity—would have been news enough, but there was more to the story: Khorloo found that the girls in these schools were fighting back.[80]

After her story was published, in both English and Mongolian, the government responded, issuing a regulation saying the practice should stop. While many celebrated, Khorloo remained skeptical. She went back the next school year to see if the practice had indeed ended. It hadn't.

As we prepared to publish a follow up story in the early summer of 2022, I had the opportunity to meet Sara Just, executive producer of *PBS NewsHour*—one of the most respected evening news shows in the United States. In a mutual friend's living room, I detailed Khorloo's reporting and the stories she had uncovered.

---

80   Khorloo Khukhnokhoi, "Female Students Revolt against 'Virginity Tests," Global Press Journal, June 2021, accessed February 3, 2023, https://globalpressjournal.com/asia/mongolia/female-students-revolt-virginity-tests/.

When I asked Just if she'd be interested in featuring the story on *Newshour* she said … yes.

In my many years of doing this, US broadcast partnerships have been nearly impossible to come by. Typically, the answer I receive is a polite no. And in truth, I had expected the same from Just.

A "no" would have made sense in this circumstance. First of all, finding minutes on the evening news for a story about Mongolia is extremely difficult. Second, the visuals of a story about virginity testing didn't exactly lend themselves to evening television. And third, Khorloo doesn't speak English. Reasons like these are why I hear "no" so often.

But for newsroom leaders who want to offer their audiences a different kind of international journalism, no isn't the right answer. Thankfully, Just agreed.

"Yes, it's challenging to do a story on a sensitive topic. Yes, it's a challenge to do a story without an English-speaking reporter involved. Yes, it's a challenge to do a story from so far away," Just told me. "But those are not insurmountable challenges when you have a good story to tell."

Say Yes

Just's yes turned out to be a very important one.

Khorloo interviewed one of the young girls on camera who had undergone virginity testing in school after the regulation to end the practice was theoretically in effect. Stephanie Sy, one of *Newshour's* reporters, interviewed Khorloo on camera, with a voiceover from one of Global Press's interpreters.[81]

The piece was a hit with viewers, did well on social media, and was shared around the world. Just a few months after the piece aired, the Mongolian government responded again. On International Day of the Girl in October 2022, the government took to Facebook, their primary communication tool with their citizens, to officially ban the practice.[82]

To date, Khorloo says the ban is truly in effect.

It may have been difficult for Just to say yes to this story, but that one word made a huge difference in the lives of girls across Mongolia. And newsroom leaders have the ability to replicate this over and over again—simply by choosing to say yes to the next great piece a local journalist puts on their desk.

Listen to Readers and Find Partners

Assuming audiences have no appetite for international news is a knee-jerk reaction. It's based on old data and old assumptions. And leaders in the newsroom would know that if they listened to their audience more carefully.

Our research and the emerging research of many others suggest that people want to better understand the world, and they want better international news.

At *PBS NewsHour*, that demand is clear. "We keep hearing from our audiences—both television and certainly our online and social media audiences—that they want more foreign coverage," Just said.

---

81 Stephani Sy and Zeba Warsi, "Virginity Testing Persists in Mongolia Despite Condemnation," PBS, July 2022, accessed February 3, 2023, https://www.pbs.org/newshour/show/virginity-testing-persists-in-rural-mongolia-despite-un-condemnation.

82 MEDS Mongolia, Twitter post, October 10, 2022, 8:28 a.m., https://twitter.com/MEDS Mongolia/status/1579629964710023168.

And finding local partners is a great way to give people what they want.

This is how Just manages to say yes to stories like Khorloo's.

"Foreign coverage is really expensive, and a lot of media outlets have scaled that back over the years that I have been in this business," she said. "There are real barriers, but finding creative ways to tell stories in other parts of the world is important. It's what really drew me to working with Global Press. I don't have the resources in public media to send a reporter to Mongolia that often, if ever."

Production collaboration, like we did with *Newshour*, is only one of the many ways newsrooms can forge such partnerships. Another option is a republishing agreement with a local newspaper in a community that your audience cares about. Major news organizations have a huge opportunity to better serve diaspora audiences with these kinds of partnerships. Global Press has numerous partners in Texas, for example, that republish our coverage from across Mexico.

When foreign to these partnerships or just relying on wire services, keep an eye on the type of international coverage you're providing your audience. Our research demonstrates that people have a desire to read comprehensive and solutions-focused news coverage about other countries and to read stories that shed light on the culture and everyday lives of communities around the world. Partnerships can open doors to reporting that leaves the sole focus on disaster behind. This is what readers want, and with the right partners, any news organization can start to deliver it.

Partnerships can also help to diversify the voices in stories.

As a professor and in speaking engagements, I am often asked my advice for young women who want a career in journalism. My answer is simple: "Take up space in systems that weren't made for you."

Obviously, Global Press's women-only reporter policy isn't right for every publication. But the lenses we use to build representative reporting teams can work for every news organization. For that to happen, though, those in charge of the newsroom have to help open up the space for greater representation.

Make It Your Duty to Care

"We need to make it clear, at every turn, that our people are more important than pageviews," Shanté Cosme, Global Press's chief content officer, wrote in an article for Harvard's Nieman Lab in 2022.[83] "To address the emotional toll of this important work, we need to offer more than performative gestures; we need to take the steps required to shift newsroom culture entirely. We need to stop normalizing exhaustion and embrace radical empathy."

She's right. It's time to move beyond the assumption that journalists are thrill-seekers or that it's simply too hard to offer the comprehensive security that all journalists deserve. Our industry needs to invest in its people.

Leadership can begin by supplementing HEFAT training with more useful options and fighting the culture of silence around mental health challenges. Journalism can be a thankless job, where risking your life to expose the truth is met with online harassment, low pay, and lifelong anxiety. The only people who can change those dynamics are those with the power to adjust policy at the top.

I'm often asked how a newsroom can get started on the path to creating a Duty of Care. I've seen great success with these three simple steps:

---

83   Shanté Cosme, "The Answer to 'Quiet Quitting' Is Radical Empathy," NeimanLab, accessed February 3, 2023, https://www.niemanlab.org/2022/12/the-answer-to-quiet-quitting-is-radical-empathy/.

- **Survey.** It's impossible for any leader to solve a problem that they don't understand. An anonymous employee survey that regularly asks questions about burnout, mental health challenges, effectiveness of current policies, and details of the primary issues plaguing the security of its workforce is essential. From there, leaders are equipped with real data to begin designing solutions.

- **Assess policies.** Revisiting newsroom policies, from expense reimbursement to time off, offers a great opportunity for leadership to investigate how security is prioritized and put into practice. A newsroom that says it cares about its people is often undermined by offering minimal time off or failing to allow for the reimbursement of lifesaving expenses that were not preapproved. With the data from your survey, you can begin making changes to those policy decisions.

- **Talk about safety.** Incorporating safety questions into the story pitch process, checking in after a difficult interview, creating group opportunities to talk about online harassment: Each of these small steps can make a huge difference to the people risking their lives, and their health, to tell stories. Creating a culture that cares and sees the whole person is worth the investment.

These are by no means the only steps required to implement a complete and more comprehensive security program. But they are meaningful first steps.

One Step at a Time

International journalism will not change overnight. But if each of us takes a few steps in the right direction, we will be closer to that reality every day.

Across the industry, many news leaders agree that this is the perfect time to introduce a more critical eye. And where old institutions lag behind, new players are already changing the game.

"I'm very hopeful for the future of journalism," Bobby Ghosh told me. "Readers have a greater awareness that our lives are connected. And so they want to understand events that are taking place far away. The old journalism institutions are not very good at swiftly responding to demand. But the new institutions emerging, they will."

I agree. But we don't have to wait for them to make progress toward that better future. The opportunities for meaningful progress are endless. We are much closer than we think. All it takes is a few steps in the right direction, and we can change our worldview and transform the entire industry—with local journalists leading the way.

Conclusion

———

The pandemic changed our world in so many ways. Most profoundly, it fostered a new sense of localization, or proximity to home.

A recent Accenture study of people across twenty countries found that the pandemic forced more than half of people to shop locally, and 79 percent of them say they plan to continue to do so over the long term.[84] We can learn a lot from the "go local" movement. It teaches us that proximity matters. Produce is fresher. We reduce our carbon footprint. We get to know the people in our community.

It's not a far cry from what news consumers are telling us they want from international journalism. They want less of the big-box narrative and more proximity—more access to real people and real stories. A fresher take on global events, in other words.

The pandemic and the racial and climate justice movements that have swirled around us for the last few years point to a future of tremendous challenge and equally tremendous opportunity. The events

---

84   Accenture, "How Is COVID-19 Changing the Retail Consumer?," August 2020, accessed February 3, 2023, https://www.accenture.com/_acnmedia/PDF-130/ Accenture-Retail-Research-POV-Wave-Seven.pdf.

of the early 2020s have caused so much suffering, but they have also reinvigorated a sense of connection.

In this moment, who tells the story matters. It has always mattered, but today it matters to readers more than ever before. It matters because people are hungry to see and understand the world differently.

Instead of parachuting in to find the most pitiful cases, we can provide a platform for a more proximate version of events. Instead of relying on stereotypes and stale narratives, we can allow local journalists to tell us the stories we most need to hear. We can employ more translators. We can share credit with fixers. And we can protect our truth tellers—the ones who risk their own physical and mental health so that we have the opportunity to better understand the world. And in doing all of this, we can also prove to our audience that we deserve another chance with their trust.

This book offers a path forward, but it is certainly not the last word on the subject. My way is not for everyone. But the incredible women of Global Press and the thousands of world-changing stories they've told over the years prove that local journalists can and should take the lead. They show us time and again that proximity and access yield extraordinary stories—and that the name on the byline truly matters.

Appendix

About the Global Press Reporters in This Book

APOPHIA AGIRESAASI is a Global Press Journal reporter based in Kampala, Uganda. She specializes in reporting on health and politics. She was part of the team named Media Hero of the Year in 2020 and 2022.

MAR GARCÍA is a Global Press Journal reporter based in Mexico City. She specializes in reporting stories that transform rote narratives about Mexican art and society. She serves as Global Press's Duty of Care liaison for Latin America. She was part of the team named Media Hero of the Year in 2020 and 2022.

KHORLOO KHUKHNOKHOI is a Global Press Journal reporter based in Orkhon, a northern province of Mongolia. She specializes in covering human rights, health, animal husbandry and cultural heritage. In 2022, Khorloo was part of a team that received a One World Media Award for their coverage of women's rights during the pandemic. She also received a Social Changemaker of the Year honor from the Stevie Awards for her powerful coverage of virginity testing in Mongolian schools that led to government reform.

MERVEILLE KAVIRA LUNEGHE is a Global Press Journal reporter based in Kirumba, Democratic Republic of Congo. Merveille specializes in migration and human rights reporting. Her 2019 coverage of the ongoing refugee crisis in DRC, "I Will Not Leave This Place," won numerous honors, including a Clarion Award for Best Feature Journalism. It was shortlisted for the One World Media Refugee Reporting Award and received an Award of Excellence from the Society for News Design.

SHILU MANANDHAR is a Global Press Journal reporter based in Kathmandu, Nepal. She specializes in migration and environmental reporting in Nepal. She has won Clarion Awards for her 2021 coverage of Nepal's stalled Truth and Reconciliation Commission and her 2018 investigation into misuse of international aid after the Nepal earthquake. She was a Persephone Miel Fellow at the Pulitzer Center for Crisis Reporting in 2015.

GAMU MASIYIWA is a Global Press Journal reporter based in Harare, Zimbabwe. She specializes in covering education and the economy. Her 2019 coverage of currencies introduced in Zimbabwe over the last decade, presented in comic form, won a Clarion Award for Best Feature Journalism.

LINDA MUJURU is a Global Press Journal reporter based in Harare, Zimbabwe. She specializes in reporting on agriculture and the economy. Her long-term coverage of the use of mercury in gold mining in Zimbabwe was featured on *PBS NewsHour* in the United States in 2022. She was part of the team named Media Hero of the Year in 2020 and 2022.

KUDZAI MAZVARIRWOFA was a Global Press Journal reporter based in Harare, Zimbabwe. She specialized in reporting on development and land reform. She was part of the team named Media Hero of the Year in 2020 and 2022. Today, she is a fact checker within the Global Press Accuracy Network.

EDNA NAMARA is a Global Press Journal reporter based in Kampala, Uganda. She specializes in reporting about power and bodily autonomy. She was part of the team named Media Hero of the Year in 2020 and 2022.

NOELLA NYIRABIHOGO is a Global Press Journal reporter based in Goma, Democratic Republic of Congo. She specializes in covering peace and security. Noella received the Ulrich Wickert Award for Child Rights for her coverage of the sexual exploitation of girls during school breaks. She is a journalist security trainer and serves as Global Press's Duty of Care liaison for Africa.

AVIGAÍ SILVA is a Global Press Journal reporter based in the Mexican state of Guerrero. She specializes in covering health and safety. She was part of the team named Media Hero of the Year in 2020 and 2022.

ALINE SUÁREZ del Real is a Global Press Journal reporter based in the state of Mexico. She studied at Technological University of Mexico. She specializes in reporting on social justice and the environment. She was part of the team named Media Hero of the Year in 2020 and 2022.

About Global Press

Global Press transforms international journalism by disrupting global narratives and promoting local access to information. By reimagining international journalism to foster global equity, we help people better understand our world.

Since 2006, Global Press has recruited and trained more than 250 reporters globally. Today, we operate independent news bureaus in more than three dozen communities across the world. Key to our success is that the reporters we recruit, train and employ are local women who are from the communities they cover. Over the last seventeen years, they have won countless awards, spurred policy change, galvanized local action, and helped millions of people to see the world differently.

Global Press was founded to reimagine international news. We know that world-class employment leads to world-class journalism. So we provide our reporters with strong wages, health benefits, industry-leading family leave, flexible vacation time, and ongoing professional development. Every team member benefits from our Duty of Care program, a holistic security system we built for local women reporters for whom, in a crisis, extraction is not an option. This program is central to our ethos and operations.

International journalism produced by local reporters enables people to pursue policy change, hold their governments accountable and make critical decisions about their lives. But in order to achieve this at an ever-greater scale, the journalism industry must elevate local journalists to report news about their own communities for local and international audiences.

When we change the storyteller, we change the story. And that changes everything.

To learn more about Global Press, visit www.globalpress.co. And to read to our news coverage visit globalpressjournal.com.

About the *Global Press Style Guide*

The Global Press Style Guide is a free online resource that establishes rules for referring to the people and places around the world where Global Press reporters work. Each entry is crafted with the specific intention of promoting dignity and precision in international journalism. Newsrooms, journalists and students are encouraged to use and implement the guide in their daily practice.

Visit https://styleguide.globalpressjournal.com/ to start using the guide today.

About Global Press News Services

Global Press News Services (GPNS) is the consulting arm of Global Press. GPNS provides consulting services to help newsrooms and NGOs establish practice change. Key services provided include a Duty of Care road map for organizations looking to build or improve their security and wellness processes and language equity services for organizations looking to improve the equity and precision in their internal communications.

Contact info@globalpressnewsservices.com to learn more about how you can work with us.